PRAISE FOR
THE UNLOCKING: AN AUTISM STORY

'*The Unlocking* is a beautiful love story from a mother to her children. It reads like a diary entry; she hopes they find it one day, which will confirm for them how much she loved them and the lengths she would go to advocate for and make the world better for both of them. It might read like a story about a boy with autism, but it is, in fact, a story about how two parents moved heaven and earth to make both their children's futures bright. It's about an amazing team of clinicians and teachers who would not let Harry's potential be unrealised. Porscia Lam's memoir serves as a roadmap for new parents feeling overwhelmed and uncertain after their child is diagnosed with autism. It's one family's story of persistence, patience and love. After reading this book, we are all on Team Harry!'

—Nicole Rogerson, CEO and founder of Autism Awareness Australia

'I found Porscia Lam's story, and her storytelling to be absolutely captivating. This book is a must-read for any parent, providing valuable insights into the challenges and triumphs that the parenting journey can throw your way.

As someone who also decided to open up to the world about his struggles, I commend Porscia for her vulnerability, honesty and self-deprecation. This raw and unfiltered account of Porscia's journey will help to normalise the struggles that so many of us deal with in our daily lives.'

—Andy McCarthy, author of *Here Comes the Sun (Affirm Press)*

'Autism can take a brutal toll on children and their families. This is a brave and honest story of persistence, resilience, and the light at the end of a very dark tunnel. I have no idea how Porscia Lam found the time and energy to write this book, but I am so very glad she did. I couldn't put it down.'

—Dr Sally Munday, paediatrician

'Porscia Lam's memoir, *The Unlocking*, is a shot of empathy straight to the heart. It's a raw, honest, and incredibly brave account of one family's journey toward an autism diagnosis for their eldest child, Harry. Set against the backdrop of Melbourne's unprecedented COVID-19 lockdowns, with Harry's behaviour escalating to self-sabotaging levels, the family teeters on the edge of breaking point. This tender, masterfully written narrative kept me turning pages deep into the night, offering a profound glimpse into the unimaginable hardships that some parents face. *The Unlocking* is a must-read for any parent, and anyone wishing to position themselves as an ally.'

—**Anne Freeman, award-winning fiction author**

'A clever and honest retelling, written with humour, joy and sadness, Porscia Lam's memoir, *The Unlocking*, vividly describes in detail her experience of having an autistic child, the all-consuming nature of a comprehensive ABA program and the difference it made for her son and whole family. ABA is sometimes considered a controversial support for autistic people however, Lam describes how it should look and how it can be compassionate, contextual and tailored to meet the needs of the individual and their family.'

— **Tineke Sibbel M.Ed, BCBA, CBA**

'Porscia Lam's memoir, *The Unlocking: An Autism Story*, is a raw and honest depiction of a mother's journey through Covid lockdowns while learning about her son's autism diagnosis. Filled with love, vulnerability and wit, Lam delivers some hard truths about not only coming to terms with what life throws at you, but learning to love and be grateful for it.

It is the type of story that grips you, shocks you, and compels you to keep turning the pages. This is essential reading for every parent, grandparent, aunt, uncle, carer, or anyone who has ever interacted with young children.

I couldn't put it down!'

—**Camille Booker, author and literary judge**

'Thank you Porscia for being a brave voice for mothers of children who are challenging or unique. Sharing such an intimate story of fierce love and real struggles makes us feel less alone. You have shown how person-centred best practice ABA can support PDA/autistic and highly anxious kids in the challenging world of neurotypicals. No doubt your story will be a gift to many in the future.'

—**Sarah Scambler, Owner/Director of Happy Oak Behavioural Consulting**

'Porscia's very personal account of her family's experiences raising autistic and neurotypical siblings will resonate with many. It's an inspiring read, especially for parents considering or already navigating early intervention strategies for their child, and likely experiencing the wave of emotions and challenges that come with a journey of this nature.'

—**Craig Salisbury, psychologist**

'This extraordinary memoir navigates the heartache and triumph of parenting an autistic child. Porscia Lam's storytelling is both poignant and uplifting as she recounts her family's journey, from a diagnosis at the height of Melbourne's pandemic, to their eventual discovery of Pathological Demand Avoidance, and the often-misunderstood world of ABA therapy. In challenging common criticisms of ABA therapy, it offers a refreshingly positive perspective on how ABA can be tailored to meet the unique strengths and needs of each child. *The Unlocking* will resonate deeply with parents of children on the spectrum while also appealing to general readers seeking a heartfelt story.'

—**Dr Erin Leif, BCBA, Senior Lecturer, School of Educational Psychology and Counselling, Faculty of Education, Monash University**

THE UNLOCKING

an autism story

THE UNLOCKING

an autism story

PORSCIA LAM

Published by The Kind Press
Copyright © Porscia Lam 2025
Porscia Lam asserts her right to be known as the author of this work.

ALL RIGHTS RESERVED.
No part of this publication may be reproduced, stored in or introduced into a retrieval system, or transmitted in any form or by any means electronic, mechanical, photocopying, recording or otherwise without the prior consent of the publishers.

978-1-7635083-2-3 (paperback)
978-1-7635083-3-0 (ebook)

A catalogue record for this book is available from the National Library of Australia.

Cover design by Christa Moffitt, Christabella Designs
Author photography by Julia Nance
Text design by Nicola Matthews, Nikki Jane Design

We at The Kind Press acknowledge that Aboriginal and Torres Strait Islander peoples are the Traditional Custodians and the first storytellers of the lands on which we live and work; and we pay our respects to Elders past and present.

DISCLAIMER
Some names and identifying details, such as physical properties, occupations and places of residence have been changed to protect individual privacy. The author provides personal experiences and insights but does not intend to, and does not, provide a substitute for professional and medical advice. Readers should seek the advice of a qualified health professional before making decisions related to their health or the health of others. To the maximum extent permitted by law, the publisher and author excludes all liability to any person arising directly or indirectly from using this book and any information or material in it.

For Harry, the star of this story, and for Tessa, who was born to steal the show.

CONTENTS

A Note from the Author	xiii
Dysfunction	1
The Plan and the Revised Plan	5
Red Flags	9
The Moment Before	19
An April Fool's Joke	23
Meltdowns	33
Living in Captivity	43
The Staircase	57
The Diagnosis	63
Pathological Demand Avoidance	77
The War in My Mind	85
Finding a Way Forward	93
The Resignation	107
The Great Observation	113
Blue Suede Shoes	129
Try Anything, But Do No Harm	139
Trick or Treat	149
When Harry Potter Saved the Year	165
The Nun	175
My Life's Great Work	185
Making Peace	195
Epilogue	201
Acknowledgements	206
About the Author	209

A NOTE FROM THE AUTHOR

While the pandemic helpfully time-stamped some historic moments in this story, my interpretation of the life events that accompanied them may well have taken on the storytelling quality and inaccuracies that come with the passage of time.

Some characters have had their names and identifying details changed to protect privacy.

This memoir is intended to be a literary work, not an academic text or a source of professional advice. It provides an account of just one family's unique experience of autism. Should you find something in here that is useful, I urge you to keep reminding yourself that many other options still exist out there. Parts of this book may upset some readers, go gently.

DYSFUNCTION

Harry carefully inspected the crumbs on his hands and began to fastidiously wipe them clean. He was five. He didn't use utensils. For almost the past three years, he had been eating only one food at dinner every night without deviation. Chicken tenders. Nothing else on the side, not a vegetable or some pasta, not even potato chips. In fact, he screamed at anything else that appeared on his plate and demanded that it be removed.

The next night, what was mildly annoying behaviour the night before had become repetitive. He would touch the chicken tender and put it down before wiping his hands clean of crumbs. He'd attempt to pick it up again, only to be faced with the same dilemma. The night after that, the wiping extended past the point where his fingers had contact with the tender. He began wiping away imaginary crumbs up to his elbows. What was repetitive had just become obsessive. In the days that followed, this behaviour continued to escalate. One night, I inadvertently brushed his hair with my sleeve when reaching across the table. Harry immediately put down his tender to grab a wet wipe, which he had requested be placed next to him, and commenced wiping the spot on his head where I had touched his hair. He then wiped all across the chest area of his tee-shirt.

Within one week from the day I first noticed his unusual wiping habit, his dinner routine had changed to involve far more wiping than eating. In the forty-five minutes we set aside for dinner, he was eating barely half a chicken tender, which he achieved only with incessant reminding and cajoling. Any kind of accidental contact between his body and the table, or himself and another person, necessitated him wiping himself from head to toe. I watched in quiet horror as he wiped down his pants and around the soles of his feet. I held my breath as he almost resumed picking up the tender, then felt a cold strike of devastation when he realised he had not wiped down the other side and dropped everything to attend to that.

I had a particular intolerance for Harry's obsessive-compulsive behaviours. A little part of me wanted to be like that, too. I had a quietly nagging urge to do unnecessary things like shampooing my hair a second time in case I didn't get everything the first or disinfecting the disinfectant bottle before I put it away. These thoughts I knew to be ridiculous and would be highly embarrassed about if ever caught acting upon them. I looked with contempt at my son as he went about unashamedly carrying out his ritual. Watching this dysfunction unfold at the table in silence was as tolerable as rubbing sandpaper across my eyeballs.

It had been three years since Harry's autism diagnosis. It was a diagnosis I had not only accepted but had welcomed with great relief from day one. However, that didn't mean I was tolerant of everything that played out because of it. *Abnormal* had become a dirty word, somehow incompatible with my best efforts to become a neurodiversity-affirming parent. Yet, right at that moment, watching him wipe himself painstakingly to the exclusion of all else, I felt I had earned the right to use it.

Harry had been having a good run recently. He often did things differently to other kids and it no longer bothered me unless the behaviour involved self-sabotage, then it roused all kinds of wretched emotions from deep within. It took me right back to the heart of Melbourne's second lockdown when everything he did was seemingly at odds with the basic tenets of the human condition. I saw Paul watching me from across the table, his face heavy with worry. Was this another passing phase or the start of a new habit? His eyes met mine, acknowledging my frustration, but he shook his head gently to bid me not to speak.

THE PLAN AND THE REVISED PLAN

When Paul and I first decided to embark upon our parenthood journey, I had a fixed idea of the type of mother I would be. Capable, modern, efficient and just a little wild. Nurturing, gentle and maternal were not words that came to mind. My own childhood, although not lacking in anything material, had lacked warmth, had been muted and businesslike. As the only child of first-generation Chinese immigrants, I was raised to be obedient and unquestioning. I handed in every piece of homework ever required of me during my entire schooling. I learnt the piano even though I hated it. I was rarely allowed sleepovers at friends' houses since sleeping outside of home could make for a loose woman, so my mother thought. My upbringing suppressed a fiery rebelliousness that would not make itself known until I finally tasted freedom and free thinking at university.

I held no attachment to childlike things and was never that fond of babies, so instead, when I thought of children, my imagination jumped years into the future where it indulged in visions of myself rock-climbing or skiing with an older child. This baby collaboration I was doing with my husband was just to get to a later stage when we could sit back and admire what a fine job we had done raising a well-adjusted individual or two.

When I fell pregnant with Harry, I had planned to return to my job as a corporate lawyer at a major bank within a year of having the baby, a plan that was disrupted upon my discovery of being pregnant with Tessa while still breastfeeding a five-month-old baby. The age gap was carelessly tight for a seemingly rational doctor-lawyer couple. I was first shocked, then embarrassed, then I sought comfort from Google to see if I was at least in good company. Perhaps this was efficiency at its finest! Britney Spears' name came up repeatedly. It seemed that similar events had conspired to send her straight into a conservatorship for the next thirteen years.

Paul was more stunned than me. His once twinkly blue eyes opened wide with disbelief. He rubbed his tired face as if to wipe away the confusion and find clarity as to how this situation could have manifested. We were still waking multiple times in the night to resettle Harry who was bafflingly becoming more difficult to care for. We hadn't even discussed having a second child and clearly had not given a moment's thought to birth control. My plan was in disarray.

I had a pervasive habit of keeping track of where my friends and peers were relative to me. I constantly monitored how I was stacking up against them. To start with, this had been a positive and reinforcing experience. At school, I was an outstanding student in nearly every subject. At university, I served on the Law Students' Society and reluctantly, owing to an underlying worrier mentality, accepted nomination as the president for which I was elected. I topped the class in contract law and was offered a job at every top-tier law firm in the country upon graduation. I came to expect enviable opportunities to simply land in my lap. I even dated well, not without errors, but definitely successfully. I had no clear vision of where I wanted to go, but it had been ingrained in me that going somewhere was important, even if I lacked authentic ambitions.

Then, right during my back-to-back stints of maternity leave, my closest friends started to achieve coveted milestones in their careers. Some were being promoted to senior management or partnership roles, or going to the bar. I had the fortune of falling in with a group of friends who were wholesome and fun, but every one of them could rightfully be considered a high achiever. I felt great pride in being in the company of these men and women with whom I had shared the experiences of young adulthood at university. They were now seen by the real world as being equipped with the skills and expertise necessary to make real decisions and close real deals. When I was hitting high notes professionally, working on billion-dollar transactions or setting up international partnerships, I had wanted to stand with them, I fit in. But after two years of maternity leave, I felt only a pulsating sense of urgency to not be left behind.

I felt smaller for watching their careers take off while my own was at a standstill. Although I was not an inherent power seeker, and secretly too much of a worrier to want to yield any true power, the corporate ladder was what I knew. It was a system for placing one foot in front of the other, to move from one moment to the next, and as a corollary, to get ahead. Until now, everything in my life had pointed me in the direction of that ladder and it had been easy enough to navigate. I had never been at my limit. I had never even had to try that hard. But all of that changed with the arrival of children.

I extended my maternity leave to twenty-four months, but it felt too long away to simply step back into the same old job when everyone else there had kept moving on and up. My reality was jarringly at odds with my focus on progress and advancement, and I remained obstinately unaware of the attitude re-adjustment I was about to receive. So, despite the bank having kept my seat warm, I resigned to take up a new job at a life insurance company beginning in 2020. I was willing to forgo the comforts of familiar surroundings, flexible work arrangements and established goodwill, in preference for starting anew. The little lie I told myself was that somehow, I had managed to keep progressing too.

RED FLAGS

Since birth, Harry had been fed a combination of breastmilk and formula. I was thankful for his willingness to easily take either since it gave me the freedom to leave him with grandparents for a few hours while I met friends at the climbing gym, and for Paul to help with an overnight feed. At about four months of age, Harry suddenly became fussy with breastfeeding, preferring a bottle, whether it be breastmilk or formula. For a few days, I thought nothing of it. When he cried for a feed but refused me, I got some expressed milk and gave it to him in a bottle.

I began researching. There was a lot of information about bottle refusal, but breast refusal was rarer. Much of the literature centred around a breastfeeding strike being a passing phase that would last a few days. Perhaps the baby was sick or teething. Perhaps I had used a new soap that Harry didn't like. Stay calm, keep trying, ride it out. After two weeks, I sought the help of a lactation consultant, but nothing changed.

In July 2018, when Harry was four months old, we flew from Melbourne to Queenstown to attend a winter wedding and enjoy a few days of skiing. I was at full milk production and alarmingly, any time Harry cried for a feed, milk spontaneously started flowing. Most mothers in this situation would simply put their baby to the breast and the problem would be solved. That solution seemed temporarily unavailable to me.

In the lead up to the flight, I mapped out the logistics of getting to Queenstown and what to do about feeding Harry. We had a three-and-half-hour flight with at least an hour of airport transit and car travel on either side, so we allowed seven hours for the door-to-door trip. That would likely be three feeds. Paul had a bottle ready for when Harry cried. At that point, I would attach the portable breast pump, throw the ski jacket over myself for modesty, hang on to the flimsy attachments of the device tightly to avoid 250ml of milk spilling into my lap, and hope that the aircraft noise would drown out the sound of my offensively groaning breast pump. It was one thing to breastfeed in public, but entirely another to express milk while sitting next to the baby that was going to drink it. We sat there as a family, Harry happily sucking down his bottle in Paul's arms, smacking his lips in satisfaction at the end, while I sat in the window seat and pumped for the next feed, making myself as small as possible under the ski jacket.

I took that pump with me everywhere on our Queenstown trip. I pumped at the wedding reception, at a winery, on the ski slopes. Every three hours, I took out all the pieces, pumped, cleaned dripping milk off myself, washed and sterilised the attachments. I got back to Melbourne and continued pumping stoically to keep up my milk supply thinking Harry would return to breastfeeding, but he never did. By the time he was six months old, I gave up. I was already pregnant with Tessa and would shortly need to do it all over again.

That was around the time I really started noticing Harry wasn't quite on the same trajectory as other babies and that perhaps the breast refusal wasn't a singular anomaly. He was my first baby so admittedly I was in uncharted territory. Paul and I had a track-record of general success in life and at the very least I considered us to be equipped with common sense. Yet we frequently found ourselves looking from the baby to the other person and uttering the words, 'Is it *us*?'

Harry wasn't vastly mismatched at first, more like a square peg that could fit into a round hole with the help of a small amount of force. We began introducing him to solid foods. He was tentative and fussy, often turning his head away at anything that looked new. He didn't like mess and anytime some mush got onto his hands he would vocalise and hold out his hand, fingers splayed in disgust, to be cleaned. We put it down to simple picky eating and continued to expose him to new foods. Over the next few years, I would read books, join online forums and consult feeding specialists about picky eating but, until we tried applied behaviour analysis (ABA) therapy at age three, the message was always the same—give him options, have a safe food available, continue exposure to new foods and textures, have shared mealtimes, make food fun.

Even in those early days, this laissez-faire approach didn't suit me. It never yielded results and I held a suspicion, based on reasons I was unable to articulate at the time, that Harry was more complicated than any solution the internet could provide. I became anxious and upset each mealtime. I was a problem solver and I wanted results. With my dogged persistence, bordering on physical badgering, Harry eventually moved on to accept small amounts of yoghurt, fruit, toast, sausages and chicken tenders. For a while I thought I had won.

By six months of age, Harry was already exhibiting a severe separation anxiety that would come to define his early years. One day he was happy being carried around by his grandparents and the next they were unable to care for him during his waking hours. He cried from the moment they reached out to pick him up and was inconsolable until either Paul or I returned or he had cried himself to sleep. With Tessa's impending arrival, we sought out the help of a nanny. We interviewed and trialled many, but the more we tried, the more distressed Harry became whenever we handed him across to one of them. Eventually, we just picked one, Bella, and tried to stick with her, hoping that the repeated exposure to one person would eventually wear him down.

For months, Bella turned up at our house to care for Harry. Even with one of us present at all times, he was unhappy, crying, back arched and hands reaching into the air, always trying to get back to Paul or me. Bella was frequently reduced to running menial errands, being asked to go upstairs and bring this and that while Harry sat glued to our laps. As he approached one year of age, Harry could only engage with Bella or the grandparents if either Paul or I were also in the room and playing along at the same game. He would grunt or cry and pull us back into that game if we tried to look at our phones or carry out some other household tasks.

The only thing that seemed to comfort Harry enough to be apart from us was giving him a bottle of baby formula and taking him for a pram or car ride. He cried and protested, sometimes with extreme distress, as he was wheeled out of the driveway, but after five or ten minutes down the road, he would eventually take his bottle and tolerate whoever's company he was in. With us no longer in sight, he was able to grudgingly take in his surroundings or watch the trains arriving and departing from the station for short periods of time. He also seemed happier to eat a small amount of food when he was cruising around in the pram or travelling in a car, distracted rather than purposefully seated for a meal in his highchair.

At some point on these excursions, he began to develop an obsessive and repetitive style of play. When he got out at the playground, rather than sit on a seesaw, he was interested in how the seesaw worked. He inspected the springs and ran from one end of the seesaw to the other. He saw other children on the play equipment but did not take a cue from them. Instead, he made them uneasy as he stood uncomfortably close to observe them in play. He didn't seem to see himself as a child. Older children sometimes offered him a place on the equipment or invited him to join in play, but he either stared back at them blankly or pointed at the equipment as if directing them to continue play while he watched on. He seemed afraid of the slide and was reluctant to sit on a swing, preferring instead to twirl himself around the A-frame of the swing or pick around in the tan bark looking for rubbish or other things that were out of place there.

Harry had no intelligible words until the age of two, but at the age of one it was clear he understood and could answer a simple question with a nod or a shake of his head if he chose to. He sometimes nodded at the suggestion of going on a train ride, but more often he wanted to just stand by the train tracks to watch the trains and repeatedly point to imperfections on the tracks while pacing up and down. At the pedestrian level crossing, he would walk onto the tracks and stand to one side of them, then the other. He leaned down and closely inspected the tracks for straightness, eyeing them all the way down the line and into the distance as far as he could see. He was oblivious to the passers-by attempting to use the crossing who had to walk off the path to get around him. If ever I tried to steer him off the crossing or pick him up to make way for people, he would protest, a low-grade whining that escalated and threatened to break into a meltdown if he was not allowed to just stand there.

I was perplexed. Harry had never avoided eye contact. In fact, he had an intrusive habit of grabbing Paul or me by the face to direct us to make eye contact with him if he didn't have one hundred per cent of our attention the very moment he demanded it. He smiled back when he was smiled at, so long as he wasn't already upset about something. He displayed animated and appropriate facial expressions with familiar people, although he often stared back blankly and unresponsively when meeting new people. If someone pointed something out to him, he looked in that direction unless he was already fixated on something else. In my rudimentary understanding, these were the hallmarks of autism and Harry didn't seem to have them.

Nothing about his appearance was atypical, either. Harry had been an objectively good looking, if scrawny, baby from day one and now he was a beautiful toddler boy. He could have been a child model with big clear blue eyes that would eventually grow hazel, a softly clefted chin, lightly chiselled features and, his great draw card, dimples that sparkled and lit up his entire face whenever he broke into a smile. From his pram, he drew compliments everywhere he went, but his behaviour was unusual. His play was odd. I wasn't even sure he was having fun. He seemed to be working, diligently performing an inspection that some unknown force required him to complete.

I was no baby expert, nor did I feel naturally maternal, and Harry's unexpected outbursts at the darnedest things shook my confidence. I was tentative about handling him or guiding him in play, lest I provoke a high-pitched squeal that turned heads all around the playground. I felt embarrassed in front of other parents and laughed off his peculiar behaviours, offering excuses or narrating his fictional thoughts aloud for others who probably found my behaviour to be overly playful and defensive.

From the time Harry was eighteen months old, I knew something was seriously wrong with his feeding. It would be some years before I came across the term "avoidant restrictive food intake disorder" or ARFID, but what I saw happen increasingly each mealtime was a disturbing and highly abnormal pattern of self-sabotage. Foods that were once an established part of his diet started to become shaky. He took his limited repertoire of foods and started to look for imperfections in them. Fruit that bore a blemish was out, as was toast with a hole in it. Chicken tenders that were not perfectly uniform in crumbing were considered broken and unfit for consumption. If a small amount of custard dripped off the spoon and landed on his tray table, it caused him to jettison the entire bowl.

Harry developed rituals where he could only suck on a yoghurt pouch if he simultaneously held the lid in his hand and played with it. I had made a habit of driving him around in the car to help him relax and feel distracted enough to eat, and I was accumulating an alarming number of near misses each time he dropped the yoghurt lid and screamed for it to be picked up from where it rolled under the passenger seat. Macaroni and cheese was either too hot or too cold. If the cheesy sauce got on his lips or chin, it distressed him. He would open his jaw to its fullest range in order to fit a tiny forkful of macaroni and cheese into his mouth without any touching his lips. I shuffled between the dinner table and the microwave to re-heat it to just the right temperature, only to find this was an unattainable moving target. At the age of one, he ate whole hash browns from McDonald's, but one day he started only eating the tops of them. He liked the crunch, but not the soft part in the middle. I showed him that the crunchy part went all along the edge of the hash brown, so he ate around the edges, getting me to flip it around for him so he could access the side within the wrapper, but he never again touched the middle part of the hash brown.

One by one he dropped established foods at the rate of one every month or two. No amount of cajoling could get him to return to them. Cutlery became playthings, a means to procrastinate so he could avoid eating. The fork became a comb for his hair, the spoon a slingshot for his peas. Sausages became toy soldiers for lining up. He rolled them around on his tray table but stopped putting them up to his mouth. I fought hard to contain my panic.

Paul sat watching me as I got up for the eighth time to heat Harry's macaroni and cheese only to have him turn his face at it.

'Just leave it,' Paul said quietly. 'You're harassing him. He's obviously not hungry.'

His voice lacked conviction. Instead, he sounded tired. He was trying to eat with one hand while pushing Tessa in her bouncer with the other.

'Well does that seem normal to you?' I asked hotly. 'He's had a bag of corn puffs and a rice cake today. All he wants is to drink milk. He clearly does not have the ability to feel hunger!'

Paul was silent a moment, perhaps acknowledging the possible truth behind what I had said. 'Well, maybe he doesn't want to eat right now, but he might later.'

'Later when? At bath time? So now we start serving heated food in the bathtub?' I asked in exasperation.

We had indeed resorted to feeding Harry in the bath. Harry engaged in play with various toys in the bath—bath paint, little boats or rubber duckies. He seemed able to eat a few grapes or pieces of mango in a setting where food was not the focus but a side distraction. Food was made into part of a game—a grape relay on the back of the duckies with the finish being when the grape got into his mouth. This was exhausting as it involved constant creativity, commentary and animation on the part of the parent supervising the bath—the very things parents have few reserves of at that time of the day. But it worked for a while, and for the foods that were hanging tenuously onto his *safe* list, I was utterly compelled to make the effort.

Eventually, it would all be in vain. Every single food that went from being able to be eaten at the dinner table to needing to be eaten in the bathtub was eventually lost. All I was doing was borrowing time, and instinctively I knew that. But I was a parent, and it was my duty to grow this little boy. I was at a loss about what else to do. He ate so little anyway, and those precious few more weeks that he might be able to cling to one more food seemed to really matter.

'I don't know, Porscia!' Paul shouted. He rarely shouted. 'Maybe you can let the bath time thing go for just one night.'

Mealtimes had become a battlefield and I fought on two fronts, one with Harry and another with Paul.

Up until that point in our relationship we had been symbiotic, but our attitude to Harry's feeding saw that break down for the first time. In Paul, I had always had a calm and unflappable partner, sometimes moody but always in control, emotions reliably dialled within a pleasant range. Everybody found him nice company. He was kind and relaxed about most things. There was a time, before the arrival of children, when my friends might have described me in the same manner, but I knew of my own potential for histrionics. It had reared its head many times in my teens when I quarrelled furiously with my mother. In an act of ultimate defiance when I turned eighteen, I had changed my birth name on a whim to spite her.

But once I had moved out of home, and throughout my twenties and thirties, I had taken great pride in my ability to project an outer calm. People praised me for my poise in all situations and I worked hard to maintain that image. I frequently sought ways to poke at this mad fiend that lay dormant within me by placing myself in situations of stress just so I could watch myself quash it. I bungee jumped, I skydived solo, I skied backcountry, I worked at the most prestigious and stressful law firm in the country and for a while, I was so well practised at keeping it at bay, nobody knew of it, not even Paul. Even I forgot about it. It was Harry who broke my cover.

I was starting to become unhinged. I was no longer able to hold a normal dinner conversation with Paul. Instead, I had become fixated on feeding Harry and the outcome of my efforts determined my mood for the rest of the evening. Paul and I argued frequently about how to deal with Harry's feeding. He was deeply troubled by it too, but was reluctant to wage the same battle against it that I was.

One night, the very last time I tried to offer Harry mac and cheese, he took a mouthful of it and gagged. It emptied the contents of his entire stomach, which was mainly his baby formula and two slices of watermelon. A food he once loved and used to request more of now repulsed him. I was devastated. We were down to only two items for dinner—chicken tenders and mac and cheese—which we alternated each night. Now we had just lost one of them. Harry didn't eat any other dinner foods and the snacks he ate during the day—corn puffs and other first foods for babies—I needed to avoid the overuse of by providing at dinner as well. He would not try spaghetti or pizza, potato wedges or chicken nuggets. Not even a different brand of chicken tender. I would have given him a bowl of chocolate custard for the sake of some variation except he had stopped eating that, too.

THE MOMENT BEFORE

It was December 2019. The world did not yet know that a global pandemic was soon to unfold. I was the mother of a twenty-month-old, still non-verbal, toddler boy and a six-month-old baby girl. The past few months had been a blur of suffering and sleeplessness. For someone who had specifically wanted the "baby phase" to be over and done with quickly, I had landed myself in an exceptional predicament.

Paul had initially taken quite well to the role of doting new father, but even he was strung out from doing it twice in such close succession and increasingly puzzled by his own apparent incompetence around Harry. He was a soft-hearted and hands-on father who willingly committed to giving bottle feeds at 2.00 am so we could split the night into shifts, even though he was working to a busy schedule as a doctor. He had sympathetically watched me perform my parenting duties perfunctorily but without much flair over the past two years. We had attempted to get our adventurous lives back on track—we went to the climbing gym together, we took the kids out on short hikes in the outdoor child carrier—but we were both exhausted and spent most of our time outdoors yawning or finding a tree to lean against.

Tessa was a terrible sleeper and Harry was simply not following the manual. He was late to walk and now extremely late to talk. We had just started speech therapy. He had, at five months of age, developed an extreme and crippling separation anxiety which, one year later, still showed no signs of abating. Both sets of grandparents who had babysat him weekly since birth suddenly could not even play with him in one room of the house while we sat in another. Either Paul or I had to be within arm's length of him or he would unfailingly and rapidly wind up in a desperate, frantic meltdown.

Shortly before I returned to working life, I went on a *mumcation*, a minibreak generously gifted to me by my husband. This was the first time I had left the kids with Paul and my in-laws to go on a three-day holiday. It had been a difficult gift to accept. I was fraught with anxiety about how Harry would cope without me, how Paul would cope with the unrelenting needs of Harry which would fall solely on him, how Tessa would fare with being hastily thrust to the grandparents most of each day, but I was effectively forced by Paul to go.

My destination of choice was Mt Arapiles, or *Dyurrite,* as it is known to its traditional owners. This hulking rock formation is three hours north-west of Melbourne with the appearance of having been dropped from the sky upon the Wimmera plains. It is a paradise for traditional, or trad, climbing—a system whereby a lead climber places natural protection using camming devices or chocks into cracks in the rock to protect from a fall, to be later removed by the following climber, ultimately leaving no trace.

I had been introduced to climbing fifteen years earlier by a colleague during my first year in a law firm. It was the elixir I needed to finally be freed from the failing but still desperate grip of my mother. As soon as I could, I learnt the skills I needed to take it outdoors. My father had been a geologist in the sixties and seventies, one of the few professional Chinese men in the Australian bush. He was such a rarity at the time that the racism he encountered in outback pubs took the form of, 'Buy the Chinaman a beer! It's good luck'. He told rollicking tales about borrowing his landlady's German Shepherd for company while he camped in a remote gorge to map its rock formations, packing his rucksack so full of dog food that he also borrowed her rifle to hunt rabbits for himself. He was forbidden by my mother from

The Moment Before

directly handing his outdoors savviness onto me, but some of it must have rubbed off anyway.

My mother detested rock-climbing and camping. She was anxious and fearful, and did not find it respectable for her daughter to be unwashed and vagrant-looking, sleeping at the foot of a mountain, only to climb up and down the thing for no apparent gain.

'Why do you like to make yourself homeless? What is the purpose?' she cried. Her objections thrust me further into the sport.

Now I was leading the second of a three-pitch climb with my longtime climbing partners Jo and Chad. Multipitch climbing occurs where a route is broken up into sections or pitches because it is too long for a standard length of rope. At the top of each pitch, all climbers meet with the gear having been retrieved by the *follower* climber, pull up the rope and reset the systems to go again. I felt surprisingly strong for someone who had given birth six months ago and another fourteen months before that, but I was nervous.

The climbing was easy, but the placement of protection was fiddly. I was out of practice having not led outdoors for almost two years. I had climbed right through both pregnancies, but only as a follower, which was considerably less risky. Now as a leader, I was unable to glance at a crack and size it up to the correct piece of gear. I would attempt to place one, find it too big or too small and fumble around with the absurd amount of metal on my harness looking for the right size, unable to recall where I had racked it.

I had always been a careful climber, but at that moment I found myself wanting to place a lot more gear than was reasonable to protect a route that I was very unlikely to fall off. I was gripping the orange rock, which had excellent friction, way too hard. A breeze that should have been delightful was just adding to the sense of airy exposure. I was seventy metres off the ground and fighting hard against the urge to downclimb back to the belay ledge and hand over the lead to either Jo or Chad. I looked down at them. They looked up at me, smiling and squinting in the sunlight, still chatting to each other, unaware of the doubt that had taken hold of me.

'You're killing this pitch,' was the casual encouragement Chad yelled up.

I found a slightly restful stance and tried to gather myself. *Imagine if Harry and Tessa were watching you! Do you really want them to see you quaking in your boots like this? Or climbing bravely on upwards like the heroine mother coming to rescue them that you always thought you would be?* My cowering on the cliff was weakness and there was no trait more abominable than being weak. My upbringing had been an austere one and I was raised to believe that weakness deserved to be punished. I was possessed by a toxic sense of ableness. My internal dialogue was hissing at me, spitting words of contempt at myself. This wasn't the kind of positive self-talk I had envisioned I would be engaging in when I left the belay ledge ten minutes earlier, but the negative beratement was strangely motivating, so I let it run.

I looked around, decided I could not hit any ledges in a fall, then pushed thoughts about the lack of protection out of my mind. I forced myself to focus on nothing but the next two moves, then two more and two more after that until I reached a large handle that allowed me to pull up around a tiny roof. Above, I easily placed a camming device, then scrambled to the ledge marking the end of my pitch and built an anchor to bring up Chad and Jo.

I had done my leading for the day and it was Jo's turn to take the final pitch to the top. The three of us squeezed onto the ledge and pulled out drink bottles and squashed sandwiches. We ate with our dirty hands and shared happy banter. Life was suddenly good again. It had been a modest climb, but in its afterglow I felt like a superhero. I could be the mother of two under two, work all week, come home to my handsome husband and scale cliffs all weekend. I was going to get more efficient in life. Nothing had to give.

AN APRIL FOOL'S JOKE

I had accepted what was originally a full-time job on a four-day-a-week basis, with the ability to work from home one day each week. Paul raised his eyebrows when he discovered I had actively convinced them I could do five days of work in four. Given that at the time I wasn't working, and we were already drowning in a sea of unrelenting needs, how did I think I was going to slide a demanding job into the mix?

When my going back to work had first been discussed in theoretical terms, we had both agreed that childcare seemed a good solution. With Harry's worsening separation anxiety, my faith in this had been wavering for some time, even before I had started applying for any jobs, but I was overcommitted to the idea and pressed ahead defiantly. Now it was evident that Paul had assumed I was just going through the job interview process as practice for when a more suitable role appeared.

I got the job, and finding ourselves in this position, we began preparing for my return to work. In December, we started with a gentle "orientation" process for Harry at a local childcare centre. The plan was that both kids would be in childcare three days a week and cared for at home the other days by a nanny and myself or Paul, who had condensed his work into a four-day week to support my career.

By mid-February, after two months of orientation where Harry was dropped off for short periods of time to get used to the childcare setting, we realised we would need another solution. For most children, two or three days of orientation are considered adequate before launching into full childcare hours. Harry had started his orientation by initially being left at childcare for just thirty minutes twice a week. We gradually extended this to three hours upon the advice of the childcare staff who promised that at a certain point he would accept the situation and calm down. At three hours, we were unable to go any further. The childcare educators were patient, reassuring and experienced with children with various behavioural challenges, but I could see they were baffled that none of their strategies seemed able to break through to Harry or lessen any of his separation anxiety.

From the time we dropped him off to the time we picked him up, he sat by the glass door, the last position from which he was able to see whoever had left him, and cried. Sometimes loudly and frantically, other times quietly or in spurts. On the days he eventually calmed down, he never moved far from that spot.

The childcare centre made daily photos available on an online parents' portal, along with descriptions of the activities and goings-on throughout the day. In all the photos, I saw Harry close by the door, sometimes hands plastered to the glass, eyes anxiously searching. Frequently, other curious children came to join him, to see what he was looking for. A cushion was placed there for him to sit on. Other children pulled their own cushions across, thinking it was a game to create a cushion mountain. But for Harry this was no game. There was never any sign of Harry engaging with others. No laughter. No dimples. His big almond eyes were either teary or distant. Not once were the educators able to report he had eaten or drunk anything. How on earth was I going to put in an honest day's work knowing this was how my son was going to pass the time whilst I was away?

Until Harry was around the age of four, we never left both children with one adult for longer than ten or fifteen minutes, even if that one adult was either Paul or me, due to Harry's propensity to unpredictably lash out at Tessa, pushing or grabbing her. The mere act of *sharing* an adult could immediately cause a behaviour escalation and heightened anxiety. He could sometimes be calm on his own, but the moment he was in a room with Tessa, he transformed into Hurricane Harry. Every object in the room, even rubbish, suddenly had ownership attributed to either one of them, usually to Harry, and there was hell to pay should one child touch another's object. Toys could suddenly not be lifted or placed by Harry. They were thrown or flung. Harry lost the ability to walk, preferring instead to crash or dramatically fall over in a chaotic mess of limbs akimbo, taking down whatever happened to be nearby.

Shortly prior to Tessa's birth, we had enlisted the help of a nanny, Luna, who built an excellent rapport with both children. Apart from us, she was the only person with whom Harry willingly and happily left the house to go to play centres or on other excursions. This allowed me to care for Tessa, who was then still on a tight feeding and napping schedule, in peace.

We were lucky to chance upon Luna in those early days. She was in her late twenties, bronzed and athletic. She ate Acai bowls and drank green smoothies. Whatever turmoil there was in her life was hidden behind the serene calm and glamour of a Byron Bay yogi. She provided us with a lot of hilarious anti-advice and off-centre observations. One day, when Paul was to sign a lease for his new medical consulting suites, she urged him, 'Don't sign today, sign later in the week. Mercury is in retrograde.' Another time, she observed the bond between me and my much-loved dog, Roxy, a border collie mix whom I had adopted nine years earlier and was more or less the dog version of me.

'Do you think you were a dog in your past life?' Luna asked earnestly.

Paul and I were two straight-thinking people. We had bonded over our shared disdain for anything resembling superstition or spiritualism. Somehow, Luna, with her hotchpotch of esoteric beliefs that seamlessly confused Hinduism with Buddhism, fit our family perfectly. Her musings were a daily blessing of unicorn dust that lightened up our tired souls and drew stifled giggles. To her, Harry was a grumpy old man stuck in a toddler's body. She would smile a generous pearly smile and Harry would smile back. He appreciated her beauty. I felt instant relief each time she entered the house, knowing that for a few hours she would take the burden of Harry from me.

We worried about relying too much on Luna. Harry required constant and involved adult engagement and if he did not get it, his persistent whining would quickly escalate into a meltdown from which it was hard to recover. It was impossible to leave Luna with both kids at once. Any suggestion that both kids play together with Luna would result in Harry dragging her away from Tessa. We feared Luna would burn through her Zen if she spent longer than a few days with him each week. We had tried many other babysitters over the months who were completely acceptable for looking after Tessa. However, they were unable to even approach Harry for a high five or with an offering of a toy without eliciting a high-pitched squeal which I could only assume meant "no".

Both sets of grandparents were eager to help cover the remaining days of the week, but my parents who lived nearby simply did not have the skills or creativity required to care for a child with such outlandish behavioural challenges. My father openly admitted to his own cluelessness. Although he liked to come around to watch the children, he was in his eighties and of very little real help. Meanwhile, my mother attempted to apply the discipline-rich approach she had once used on me as a child to Harry, thinking his behaviour stemmed from an oversupply of fun and a lack of seriousness from us. The state of my relationship with my mother was such that it gave me equal parts maddening frustration and deep satisfaction to watch her attempts at discipline backfire spectacularly in her face each time, and yet she would attempt the same thing again and again.

This left Paul's parents. They were modern and fit and, both being retired schoolteachers, approached Harry's behaviour with a level of understanding which enabled them to somewhat successfully care for him for short periods, so long as we were around for reassurance. They came armed with gadgets and toys that featured buttons and levers, a fascination of Harry's that seemed to satisfy an intense need to fidget and fiddle. Harry blew hot and cold with them but, most days, always after an initial period of resistance and desperate clinging onto either Paul or me, they were usually able to convince him to go out to a playground or on a train ride. So, with a roster of in-home help hastily cobbled together, we pulled both Harry and Tessa out of childcare. It would be mayhem with both kids at home. We would need both Luna and Paul's parents at the same time on the days we were both working, but it looked to be a workable solution. At this stage, I still believed I would be in an office three days a week, enabling me to leave the chaos of the household behind.

1 April 2020 was my first day of work as a senior lawyer at the life insurance company. After two years out of the office, three weeks earlier, I had enthusiastically purchased a new work dress to mark the occasion. How the world changed in those three weeks. What had begun as a distant virus sweeping through China in mid-January and February had now reached our shores, embedded in Melbourne and was advancing around the state.

I had initially dismissed the fuss over COVID-19 as a gross overreaction. Reports indicated that most infected people suffered mild flu-like symptoms with severe cases mainly seen in the elderly and vulnerable. My mother was a hypochondriac and therefore I abhorred hypochondria. I thumbed my nose at the threat. Surely this would just follow the same trajectory as the 2003 SARS pandemic which had spread to only a handful of countries and was resolved a few months later.

By mid-March, the COVID-19 outbreak had become a full-blown

pandemic and was making headlines throughout the day with minute-by-minute updates on the changing situation. Countries in Europe, where the disease was more widespread, had started imposing restrictions on movement. Victoria had just declared a state of emergency under public health laws, allowing the government to exercise all sorts of unprecedented emergency powers. International borders were closed to all except returning Australian citizens and permanent residents. Restrictions of mass gatherings had been put in place to slow the spread of the virus and avoid overwhelming the hospital system. Case numbers in Victoria rose from the 200s to just below 1,000 in the last two weeks of March. As parts of the world began to enter lockdown, Paul looked at me.

'Do you really think you're going to be able to start work in two weeks? Maybe you should ring your boss and see if they will push your start date back until this blows over?' he asked.

His casually phrased question betrayed a hint of hopefulness. Paul was supportive. He hadn't liked watching me fester through maternity leave, but he had really hoped I would find a lesser role. He harboured, and rightfully so, serious concerns about how we would be able to both fulfil our work duties and parent two children under the age of two, one of them displaying increasingly peculiar needs and attachments. The word *autism* continued to hang weightily over us, but was still not seriously entertained. Harry was playful and sought constant engagement from his trusted adults. He wasn't closed off to us, even though he did seem to be somehow incompatible with everyone, as if we were speaking English and he was speaking Latin. We were aware that there was a problem of sorts, but this still wasn't quite what either of us recognised as autism in our limited understanding of the subject.

'I'll call him and check what the plan is for the first day,' I said.

I was now reading news reports of companies requesting all staff to work from home, and of offices in Melbourne's central business district undergoing deep cleaning after the identification of an infected employee.

'I think we still go ahead as planned. I'll have Rebecca get in touch to organise your building pass,' came Mike's assured response.

Mike was to be my boss. He managed a legal team that was spread across Melbourne and Sydney from a swanky new office in Melbourne's corporate Docklands precinct. I had met him over the course of three interviews. He exuded such confidence and calm that I felt no need to plan for an alternate scenario.

On 31 March, Victoria entered the first of what was to eventually be six lockdowns. Stay at home orders were issued and Stage Three restrictions were introduced. Under those restrictions, there were only four reasons people were permitted to leave their house for—food and supplies, exercise, medical care and work or education where work from home was not possible. Visitors were no longer allowed in the home. Gatherings of more than two people outdoors were banned. All non-essential services were banned. Rebecca's email outlining the process for me to enter the office arrived later that day.

Please be ready to have your pass photo taken. It will last your entire career at the company, it read in an upbeat tone. Rebecca was the bubbly executive assistant to the team, and she was located in Sydney which was not subject to a lockdown at the time.

Thanks for letting me know a few hours too late, I replied. *I would have booked a haircut, but all Melbourne salons are locking down within the next two hours.*

Later still, a call came from Mike. Things were evolving quickly.

'Let's meet at 9.00 am tomorrow for you to collect your laptop and get onboarded. Then you will need to work from home for the rest of the day,' he said, sounding a little flat now. 'The office is empty. Everyone has just been ordered to work remotely.'

I arrived for my first day at work. I was wearing my new sage-green corporate dress and a pair of taupe pumps. For the first time in almost two years, I had blow-dried my hair and applied lipstick, which I had never done before, even in my working prime. I've always had a thing about efficiency. I wanted to look good enough, but not *so* good that I wasted time I could spend doing something else.

My heels clicked across the shiny lobby floor. I had strangely missed this sound, but now that the expansive lobby was completely empty except for one security person, the sound of my heels seemed to take over the entire space. I walked past glossy black columns leading to an atrium. Metal trimmings smartly accentuated the floor to ceiling windows. When I had arrived in this building for the first of three job interviews, I imagined one day taking Harry and Tessa here on a bring-your-kids-to-work day and impressing them with views of the waterfront from Mummy's work. Now, the five glistening, interconnected office towers felt like a deserted theme park. I rode an escalator up to where the multiple high-speed lifts stood. I rose slowly above a lower tier of closed and empty restaurants, cafes, supermarkets and shops.

I arrived at the elevators. A paper sign read, *One person per lift.* These new high-speed elevators required me to press the number of the floor I wanted to go to, then a screen lit up, directing me to the assigned lift. It was a means of sorting large numbers of office workers into groups for efficient travel depending on how high they were going up in the building. Today it was just me. I got into a spacious lift that could easily fit twenty people and saw my own smart reflection as the doors closed. I had overdressed for the apocalypse. I had received the memo about lockdown but hadn't considered the dress code.

At reception, one person still staffed the desk. He had been waiting for me, the unfortunate new starter.

'So, you're the April fool!' he said, grinning at the sight of a person. He took my photo and issued the pass. Soon, Mike came to meet me along with Jim from the technology team who was carrying my new laptop and phone. We greeted each other, standing further apart than normal in polite society, and had a quiet chuckle about the situation. Handshakes were firmly off limits.

In the early months of the pandemic, people awkwardly began adopting the new government-mandated practice of social distancing. This was new vocabulary that would soon encompass a range of acts, including the ungainly substitution of hands for elbows to carry out tasks like pressing buttons, and standing one-and-a-half metres apart. Mike and Jim appeared dressed to undertake some weekend chores in tee-shirts, jeans and sneakers. They led me to the open plan workspace where desks were arranged in pods for collaborative working. Hundreds of laptop-docking stations stretched across the empty floor. A whiteboard filled with balloons and arrows marked the efforts of a brainstorming session, a sign there was once life and business conducted here.

'So, when did all this happen?' I asked, gesturing to the vacant floor.

'Yesterday the email came through directing everyone to work from home from now on unless there's a specific exemption. So, right now, that's us,' replied Jim grimly. 'Last week you could see it coming, though. The city was clearing out.'

Just then, Mike looked up from reading an alert on his phone with a wry smile.

'I just got a reminder because last week I blocked out some time for your welcome lunch at 12.00 pm. We should still grab a bite after this.'

There were one or two cafes downstairs still operating, but they were now permitted to serve takeaway only.

'Fantastic,' I said. 'I'll order the most expensive thing on the menu.'

What followed over the next hour was a socially distanced interplay between Jim, Mike and me. We sat just beyond arm's length apart, sanitised our hands, logged onto the laptop, entered a password, wiped the keys using a disinfectant wipe, passed it onto the next person to reset a new password, wiped the keys clean using a disinfectant wipe and then passed it onto the next person to set up the application. Sometimes this didn't work, and we had to do it all over again until my laptop was finally set up. We stopped for a takeaway sandwich, my welcome lunch, then we repeated the process with the phone. By the time this was all done I was starting to think like a hypochondriac. When I had packed up my new items, we bid farewell to each other and I left the empty office to finish the day and start my new career working from home. That was the last time I ever saw the office.

MELTDOWNS

Week two on the job and week two of lockdown. I glanced at the calendar on my laptop and saw three hours of online meetings scheduled for the day. I was doing my best to set up my days so that as many of the meetings as possible took place either first thing in the morning or later in the afternoon, both times when Harry was usually out of the house. Realistically, the two hours in the middle of the day when both kids were in the house for lunch and naps was a working wasteland as they both vied for my attention.

Harry's complete lack of recognition of the concept of sharing, even in an unstructured sense, and low frustration tolerance resulted in frequent physical altercations with Tessa. He would lunge to pull Tessa off my lap to make way for himself. He could not accept me having one arm around him and another around Tessa. He refused to see me as a shared resource when Tessa, fourteen months younger, had the understanding of fairness and the tolerance to accept that.

Once, with little warning, he lashed out and scratched her across the face when I attempted to cuddle them simultaneously under an arm each. Tessa, a bouncy, happy baby, screamed in pain as three angry red welts immediately rose on her forehead and plump pink cheeks. Harry showed no cognition to the pain he had caused. He was not stunned by her cries. He did not pause. He looked straight at Tessa and continued, undeterred, to try to wrestle me away from her. It startled me. I could not help but compare. Even Tessa, not quite one year of age, could show concern for someone else's cries of pain. Sometimes the sight of Harry crying would cause her to cry. Harry's apparent lack of empathy troubled me.

To further add to my difficulties, it was frequently impossible to start working until close to 10.00 am if the grandparents were helping out, due to the fact that Harry required a gradual warm-up and handover involving my careful mediation of games of peekaboo or hide and seek before he was accepting enough of Nana and Pa's presence to leave the house with them.

The situation was better on the days that Luna came. Harry would happily follow her out the door, making a range of "gar gar" and "eew ooo ooo" sounds and gestures to which she responded. She was completely present in his world. She may not have understood every sound he made, but she validated his world as the only one that was real for the time she was there. She gave him one hundred per cent of her attention. He was satisfied. We asked nothing of Luna other than to be available for Harry. She was not required to do any household chores. For me, it was already the greatest gift each time he left the house with her, giving me a few precious hours to work. I watched their two silhouettes walking down the hallway and out the front door, hand-in-hand, engaged in a fluent back and forth of English and gibberish.

The Stage Three restrictions Victoria was subjected to that first lockdown brought an end to all gatherings, with the exception of two people outdoors. School holidays had been brought forwards by a week and school-age children were now at home to reduce the spread of the virus. The use of childcare continued to be allowed, although the lockdown rules were silent on the use of in-home nannies.

Over the course of the next two years, Victorians would become exceptionally well-versed in the language of lockdowns and the public health orders that were used to give effect to six of them. They would come to know that under Stage Three restrictions all non-essential retail was closed, weddings were limited to five guests, but childcare and kindergartens remained open to all. Under Stage Four restrictions, childcare and existing in-home care arrangements were only permitted to children of essential workers, movement restricted to a five-kilometre radius of one's home and weddings banned. However, the first set of orders were untested and hastily released to a stunned community with a plea to do the right thing. Details were highly specific in some places but scant in others. At all times, an exemption to the restrictions was included for care and compassionate reasons, which included disabilities.

I had a mounting list of matters needing urgent attention at work and I felt the first pangs of panic as I sat there spending my limited time reading and re-reading the public health orders, trawling through each line. Were we permitted to use an in-home carer for Harry? I was skilled at reading such things, but I couldn't find the answer. As a doctor, Paul was an essential worker, and although much of his consulting work was being conducted remotely, he was still physically required to be in attendance at the hospital on most days for procedures. I, like nearly every other office worker, was constrained to working from home and the orders were silent as to whether a nanny was allowed, although the spirit of them seemed to suggest "no" since they were aimed at preventing members of different households from mixing.

Around the time I returned to work, we received confirmation that Harry had been accepted onto the National Disability Insurance Scheme, or NDIS, on the basis of a diagnosis of Global Developmental Delay, allowing him access to government funding for early intervention services. He had not yet been diagnosed as on the autism spectrum and, as a result, we did not strongly identify as being a part of the disability community.

The process of obtaining a diagnosis of autism was a lengthy one, requiring the joint opinions of a paediatrician in conjunction with a multidisciplinary team. In Harry's case, this would be a psychologist and a speech pathologist. In November the previous year, we had begun seeing paediatricians, seeking advice on how to deal with Harry's rapidly escalating behavioural challenges. The word autism had been suggested as a possible explanation. Harry had special interests which were obsessive and repetitive. He often honed in on minor details, but his strong attachment to Paul and me and his ready eye contact still threw off the initial paediatricians and psychologists. Separation anxiety and generalised anxiety were the favoured explanations and at only eighteen months of age at the time, no one was pushing us towards an autism diagnosis. However, his extreme anxiety, in combination with his lack of intelligible words and poor emotional regulation, was enough to earn him a diagnosis of Global Developmental Delay.

I considered GDD to be a holding diagnosis for a child being not-quite-right, but with no one able to precisely point the finger at what was wrong, or provide a clear strategy on how to move forward. It didn't seem to hold the gravitas needed to be brandished about as a real disability, but it gave him the status of a participant under the NDIS, and that gave us enough confidence to use the care and compassion exemptions which allowed someone from another household to provide in-home care. What we could no longer justify was having both Luna and Paul's parents around to keep the kids separated while we were working, as we had originally planned.

Still, the situation had been salvaged for the moment. I wasn't going to be highly productive, but nor was anyone else working from home with a child. Play centres, libraries and even playgrounds were closed, but Harry was at least able to go on pram rides and walks to the park, pick flowers and chase the birds. I felt relief that Tessa would have a few hours safe and away from Harry. She was still young enough to be satisfied with some distracted care while I was haphazardly working, so long as Harry wasn't around.

With the exception of Mike, I hadn't met any of my colleagues in person. However, during our online meetings, I met not only them but their assortment of pets, partners, housemates and children. Many children popped up unannounced during online meetings to have a look at the screen, sometimes pressing a button or two and then wandering back out. Once, a child of around six or seven years of age ran up to his father in front of the computer waving his underpants in clear view of the camera to let him know he had had a toileting accident requiring urgent attention. Colleagues dialled in from the unlikeliest of working locations in their homes—one sitting on the washing machine since that week the laundry was his office while his wife had the study. This was the new way of working in 2020. Everyone had a chuckle and carried on with business. We were lucky to be working at all.

What played out in my house, however, seemed to be a little bit extra. Trouble would arise if Harry returned home for his lunch and nap, and I had the misfortune of still being tied up on a video call. As soon as Harry came home from an outing, he urgently set about trying to locate me, knowing the study was the most likely location. I usually had the study door closed, but could hear him coming up the stairs. If I wasn't in a meeting, I normally took that as a cue to wrap up work for the morning and have lunch with him. But if I was on a call, I kept the door closed and my headphones on, hoping for just a few extra minutes' grace from Harry so I could finish the call.

'Mama's working,' I heard Luna explain to him.

'Gar gar,' Harry replied, probably pointing at the door and gesturing for it to be opened.

'Let's go down and have some lunch. Mama can join us when she's finished.'

'Gar gar!' louder and more pressing this time. I could hear him brushing against the door, on tiptoes, trying to reach the handle. Then banging, smacking the door.

If I didn't have headphones on, the noise from Harry would now be enough for everyone in the meeting to hear, but I kept my headphones on and concentrated on maintaining my listening face. My laptop screen was divided into six rectangles, with a colleague's face framed within each of them.

'Porscia is across the Sale and Purchase Agreement,' came Mike's voice over the call. 'She can talk to that.'

Until now, Harry knew I was in the office but had not yet heard my voice. I braced myself. I had no choice but to speak.

'Yes, in the original agreement, that is addressed as a covenant …' I said, with deliberate calm. Violent banging on the door ensued. '… but not as a condition precedent.'

Harry's "Gar gar!" was now turning desperate.

'Gar gaaaaarrr!'

He now knew for sure I was inside and was frantic to get to me. Luna must have peeled him off the door, only for him to run back and slap his body loudly against it.

'Uh-uh, Harry, no hitting,' I heard Luna say firmly but gently. I could no longer maintain my train of thought.

'In the second amendment, this was changed to include it as a condition precedent,' I struggled on.

'Mama! Mama! Gar gar! Gaaaar!'

Oh my God! I think he just said mama! But it wasn't a moment to be savoured.

In less than three minutes, Harry's low-level whining had escalated into a full meltdown. These ferocious meltdowns were quite different to tantrums. They used to happen once every few days, but lately had become a daily, sometimes twice daily, occurrence. Even if I now opened the door to let him in, the situation was irrecoverable. Yet I couldn't let Luna deal with this on her own. Fifteen minutes of this would be enough to fry anyone's brain. She would surely quit.

'Do you need to attend to something?' asked Mike kindly. Mike had school-age children of his own and had either noticed the shaking of the door behind me on the video, or perhaps I had unwittingly dropped my working face.

'Sorry. My son's having a meltdown. I'll try letting him in. It's possible he may not let me speak. If that's the case, perhaps I can send a note around after this meeting to cover off this point.'

Mike nodded. I opened the door. Harry burst through crying, arms flailing, in turns lashing out at me then pulling at my clothes, indicating he wanted to be picked up. I picked him up. I tried to sit him on my lap in front of the computer and put my headphones back on. I pointed to the screen where my colleagues waved at him and smiled at me sympathetically. He normally liked to look at screens, but not today. He pulled my headphones off and threw them on the ground. He grabbed my face savagely and tried to turn me away from the screen. He didn't want my attention to be elsewhere.

Desperately, I tried again to draw his attention to one of the faces on the screen. Mary was holding up a teddy bear to her camera. I tapped at her on the screen, not because I thought it could possibly help, but because I felt I owed it to my colleagues to at least look like I was trying. Harry reached out to slam the laptop shut. His face was purple and glistening with tears. I held him back, frustrating him more. He was thrashing about on my lap like a freshly reeled marlin. I released him. He shot out of my arms and swiped the laptop off the desk, sending it crashing to the ground. Now he pointed at it on the ground, directing me to pick it up. I walked over to pick it up. He grabbed it and threw it back down, then pointed to it again. I was stuck in the dreaded loop with Harry. This happened often in meltdowns. I would attempt to do what I believed he was asking me to in order to pacify him. But, either I grievously misunderstood what was being demanded of me, or at that point nothing could be carried out to his satisfaction and every failed attempt to do so served only to inflame his anger further.

With the meeting aborted, I put my full attention towards trying to calm Harry. I spoke to him in low, calming tones, but any word coming out of my mouth prompted another fresh barrage of wails. Frazzled, I looked at Luna who had been standing just outside the study door, watching helplessly.

'Can you grab one of his garbage trucks from downstairs?' I asked.

She left quickly and returned with the truck a minute later, now carrying Tessa who had heard the ruckus upstairs and was attempting to crawl her way up to see what was going on. Harry grabbed the truck and threw it, narrowly missing Tessa who immediately began to cry in fright. I gestured for Luna to take her away. Now I sat there on the ground in silence as he stood next to me, feet planted apart, gasping and crying but otherwise unmoving, arms held stiffly to his side slightly away from his body. Perhaps I could sit it out and eventually he would calm down. Minutes passed and the meltdown showed no sign of abating. He wasn't even getting hoarse. I tried looking at him. I tried looking away. It made no difference. I got to my feet to walk away, perhaps to sit just outside the door and give him some space. This movement sparked an escalation, a higher level of frenzy in his cries, so I sat back down. He returned to the same rhythmic gasp and cry as before.

With close to thirty minutes having elapsed since the meltdown started, and unable to take the wait-it-out approach any longer, I desperately scanned the room to see what could be used to distract Harry and snap him out of this brain freeze. I opened drawers and futilely offered a large calculator which briefly stalled his wails but ultimately proved insufficient. A hole punch. A pack of highlighters. Eventually, at the back of one of the drawers, I inexplicably found a handful of balloons, not yet inflated. He had never seen a balloon being inflated before. I gave it a go. I blew into one and he immediately stopped crying as he saw it begin to inflate. I blew again. It got bigger and he continued to watch. As suddenly as the meltdown had started, it was over.

I was trembling with adrenaline. Blood pulsated loudly in my ears. Harry, now calm and playing with the balloon, allowed me to pick him up and take him downstairs. He was hot and sweaty. I talked to him softly about how we were going to have some lunch, maybe some cheese and fruit toast, things he still ate at the time. I got to the living room couch and set him down to go and prepare lunch. He continued to lean heavily on my arm as I tried to extricate it from beneath him. I looked and saw his eyes were half-closed, not quite asleep, but his little face was peaceful. He was still at last.

I understood the small child slumped against me had called none of the shots in what had just unfolded. Some other invisible, powerful, all-consuming force had just materialised out of thin air to possess him, then left as abruptly as it came. I brushed the last streaks of tears off his cherubic cheeks and hugged him gently. We sat together and bathed in the post-meltdown peace.

LIVING IN CAPTIVITY

By mid-May the number of coronavirus infections in Melbourne had fallen significantly and restrictions from the first lockdown started to ease. Work from home orders continued for office workers but by June, playgrounds, play centres and shopping centres reopened, making it easier to keep the kids out of the house for longer periods. For a brief time, I had a taste of life as a functioning but hectic working parent. It was certainly less fun than what I had in mind and now that I was working from home indefinitely, far less glamorous. My fashion sense took a hit from which it never fully recovered as I rotated between three or four combinations of tee-shirts, sweaters and leggings. I tied my hair up but only finger combed it for the rest of 2020. I was surprised by the ease with which I became slovenly.

In reality, my four-day working week was spread out day and night over every spare minute of the entire week while I tried to make myself available to the kids as much as possible. On the days when Tessa and Harry spent too much time in the house together and broke out in repeated fights, I was forced to take an active role in their care, blocking out my work calendar to take one of them out. But with the simultaneous use of both Luna and my in-laws, I was able to patch together a modest day's work.

I felt great relief when the climbing gyms reopened in June, and eagerly met up with friends. None of my climbing partners had kids and simply could not relate to my ordeals over the past few months, but it was a welcome change to be with them. We chatted about fun and frivolous things. We spoke dreamily of future climbing trips. The movement of climbing provided me with a meditative kind of peace I had never been able to achieve in the handful of times I attempted actual meditation. There was something about the intensity of stillness, the lack of movement, that felt claustrophobic. Nothing called my impatience to the helm faster than when I had to mindfully count backwards from ten to zero while exhaling. I simply couldn't help but start working on to-do lists in my head for the very moment I was set free. Yet with climbing, I was moving and going somewhere, but nowhere important, so I was fully consumed in that moment. That time on the wall was the only time in my waking hours when I wasn't worrying about how to feed Harry or whether I really had to attend all the meetings scheduled for the following day. It was a little pocket of sanity.

Fortuitously, I also seized upon this moment to commence an autism assessment while some non-urgent health services had returned to face-to-face appointments. Since November, every few weeks or so, Harry had seen a child psychologist for his anxiety and a speech pathologist for his language delay. He had made some inroads in his speech and was able to use sign language to communicate basic requests as well as uttering a few words like "mama", "dada", "off" and "go" with meaning. We had sought the opinions of two paediatricians by this time. The first conducted extensive blood tests to check for chromosomal abnormalities and rule out other organic causes, but failed to grasp the full extent of our difficulties or recognise that the two intelligent people standing before her were completely out of ideas on how to get their two-year-old to put on a sunhat. The second felt his behaviours were largely explained by his anxiety. Autism was discussed but Harry was still very young for such a diagnosis, with the average age of an autism diagnosis in Australia being over four years. None of the professionals really seemed to *want* to go there yet.

Desperate for a more satisfying answer, Paul took Harry to a third paediatrician in May who recognised something we had not yet managed to put a word to: his *inflexibility*. He was two years and two months old at the time of that appointment. Yes, he did engage in play and he did seek attention from people, but it was all on his terms. She observed that Harry needed to hold Paul's hand the entire time of the appointment and demanded a strict routine about when Paul was allowed to let go of his hand. When the routine didn't go as planned, Paul had to retrace his steps and do it all over again in the manner required. This rigidity was mirrored in many other situations, such as when Paul could join in his play or put a hat on. For clarity, I am talking about Paul's hat, since no way was Harry wearing a hat! Harry would not tolerate the sight of anyone wearing a facemask, an aversion that would inconveniently last the entire pandemic. He required Paul and the paediatrician who were both wearing them to remove them. I read her report: *The question of autism has been raised in the past, and at first glance Harry does tick some of the boxes, but there is no need to rush into a diagnosis at the moment.*

During this time, I had started reading articles about autism secretly but voraciously, completing online questionnaires to see if Harry met the criteria. Within the first few days of working from home, I had tentatively reached my own conclusion that he was on the spectrum. In recent years, I have read articles that indicate a high level of accuracy in parents who hold early suspicions that their child is on the spectrum, their observations later confirmed by an affirmative diagnosis. Paul had been wracked with indecision about whether to seek the diagnosis at such a young age, wondering if it might sentence Harry to a life of discrimination, a label that would limit his opportunities in later life. I did not share his hesitance and could only feel the sense of urgency that hung in the air. I already knew the answer, but I wanted it in writing. A diagnosis of ASD rather than GDD would give Harry access to a large array of services offered by autism providers and would likely increase his funding under the NDIS.

Lockdown had lifted but the situation was precarious. Health services were backlogged and overwhelmed. Only one of the psychologists Harry had been working with was qualified to conduct an autism assessment and he was shortly to relocate to another state. It would significantly speed up the process to go through a psychologist that Harry was already known to. This was a window of opportunity. I was both impatient and opportunistic and had a reputation at work for getting things done. I argued my case to Paul and won. I called all of Harry's specialists the next day and requested the assessment process to begin.

By the first week of July infections were on the rise again. What had started as a cluster of cases resulting in a lockdown order for several western suburbs in Melbourne resulted in a rapid rise of the virus throughout metropolitan Melbourne. On 8 July 2020, the city was back in lockdown. Stage Three restrictions were reintroduced. This time, disability support groups were prepared and released explanations about how lockdown exemptions could be used for those with disabilities, including the receipt of in-home care. We would again lose the luxury of having separate carers for each child, but at least could continue to have someone take Harry out of the house. Tessa, who was now one year and two months old, would again be cared for by me, or Paul when he wasn't working.

A week later, all the people we were relying upon to hold this delicate situation together vanished. Luna, who had been with us for over a year, failed to turn up one day. I texted asking if she was running late and got a reply. *I can't do this anymore. I'm really sorry. I'm not able to look after Harry when I need to look after myself first right now.* She didn't answer my call, so I texted her back. *Are you okay? Is this because of lockdown, or because of how difficult Harry has been? Is it Adam?* I knew she was in a tempestuous relationship. Perhaps they had fought, and she was still smarting from that. She had a complicated family situation. Maybe something from the lockdown had stirred up memories from her past. The carefree yogi-like calm she projected was a front that concealed complex insecurities. I had readily sensed that since I had a front of my own, but hers had been so carefully curated, presented so authentically, and suited her with such perfection that it still shocked me to see it crumble.

I reflected on the past few months with Luna. I had noticed that Harry's level of difficulty had escalated over the course of the first lockdown. He had started refusing to go out with Luna for a walk, possibly because playgrounds were closed. We were avoiding using public transport, so train rides had ceased, too. There was no incentive for him to leave the house and he had developed an intense dislike for putting on his shoes. He instead preferred to play with Luna in the cubby house we had built in the backyard during that first lockdown. Luna knew how much I wanted him out of the house. I was working from home every day, he knew where to find me, and find me he did every few minutes. He wanted to show me things he had found or drag me over to admire the blocks he had stacked. I was exasperated. He had a dedicated resource in Luna, but she wasn't enough. Reading insurance legislation was a challenge at the best of times and with Harry around, I wasn't even getting a clear ten minutes to do that.

His refusal to leave the house affected his relationship with Luna. She felt pressure from me to get him out, and she felt disappointment that his affection towards her had cooled. In the break between lockdowns, she had erratically cancelled a few of her scheduled days and then asked for a week off, sending me into a frantic search to find a fill-in nanny. I sensed something was awry. Her heart wasn't in it anymore and she had lost her connection with Harry. Something in her own life was consuming her. She was a registered support worker under the NDIS, and I can only guess that she found an easier family to provide care for during the lockdown. But I never found out the reason she quit.

Paul was angry. He took the day off work to care for Harry that day. There was no other option and he recognised it was unsafe for me to care for them both the entire day, even if I wasn't working. Neither of us had attempted to do that on our own before. It had never even been possible for one of us to take both children across the street holding one child in each hand. The very words "one hand each" would have been enough to induce Harry to grab both to stop Tessa getting one, or demand to be picked up.

'I'll get my parents to pick up an extra day,' Paul said. 'Maybe I can drop a day at work while this lockdown continues.'

Then came the second blow. Two days later, Paul's parents announced they had decided to isolate and were no longer prepared to continue looking after Harry. They reasoned that Paul was high-risk due to his work in a hospital setting and that Paul's dad was vulnerable due to a pre-existing heart condition. Now I was angry.

Anger, disappointment, despair. These were the emotions that descended upon our household in the early days of that second lockdown. Winter had just arrived. Two out-of-control children had just emptied the bookshelf of every book within their reach, scattered the contents of all the drawers in the kitchen onto the ground and broke up the printer into its separate component parts. Their two depressed parents set about cleaning this up while feuding about who needed to quit their job first.

It was our first proper fight, but we didn't look like amateurs. I don't remember much of what Paul said, but I recall the vitriol with which every word was ejected from my mouth. My mad fiend who had lain dormant for over fifteen years was back. Paul was disappointed but he defended his parents' decision, and I was angrily yelling at him for it. Why was I yelling at him? The decision had been made and it was his parents' to make. He had taken no part in it.

I was acutely aware of my misplaced sense of entitlement. I had wrangled to keep a lid on my frustrations, but they had escaped and were making a crazed dash to get away. In the moment, frustration turned to fury and left my mind with no place for reason. Paul's insistence that his parents were choosing to do this so they could be around to help us in the future only enraged me further.

The topic of Paul's parents became such a sensitive topic that we tried to avoid mention of them for the rest of the year lest it ignite another battle. When they called him, I would fall into a sulky silence. It was the best I could offer to not inflame the situation. With Luna and Paul's parents out of the picture, I had no option but to turn to mine. For all their incompetence as babysitters and my stormy relationship with my mother, they were still eager to help. I reasoned that they were at least adults who could monitor the kids and call out to me in the next room when it got out of hand.

My father was eighty-five at that stage and had a knack for falling asleep within minutes of sitting down. He had poorly controlled diabetes and could rarely even hear the kids fighting, so I really couldn't trust him to do much at all. He was mainly reduced to cuddling Tessa on the couch or shielding her from Harry. My mother lacked the listening skills to take in instructions about the kids, particularly the complicated and seemingly arbitrary ones for Harry. Typically, I would begin explaining the routine to her and halfway through my explanation I could tell she thought she had it worked out. She would begin nodding knowingly, 'uh-huh, uh-huh, hmmm', and I could see in her eyes she wasn't listening anymore. Exasperated, I began asking her to repeat my instructions back to me.

'You can start by giving him the train tracks to play with. At 10.30, he has a snack break. Give him his fruit pouch. You will need to take the lid off for him but give it back to him to play with it. Can you please say that back to me?'

'Ah, yes. Give him train tracks at 10.30. He gets a fruit pouch for the break. Give him something to play with.' She failed to grasp that it was the minor details that would make or break the situation.

Having my mum supervise the kids for extended periods was simply unworkable. Every thirty minutes or so, Harry broke into a meltdown when she was unable to follow instructions, or she moved his special toy that he had seated just so. She lacked the intuition to effectively improvise. I knew she was taking a risk by coming to help us, a noble act of love in the circumstances that I should have felt gratitude for, whatever her performance. Yet I watched her go about the day oblivious to her own incompetence, filled to the brim with an astounding but unfounded confidence in her own abilities, and all my childhood vexations reared up angrily before me.

I had just started a new job three months ago and I was not prepared to quit and carry that kind of blemish around on my resume after two years of parental leave. Paul knew he had no choice.

'I'll take leave from the public hospital for the next few months. All the lists have been cancelled anyway,' he said quietly a few days later. 'I'll just consult from home a day a week and maybe we can try to find another carer ... I don't know how we even hire someone right now.'

I didn't thank him for it. I was still too disgruntled and disappointed about everyone around us to be able to express gratitude.

Paul became the primary carer. He conducted some telehealth consultations from home for his private patients, but most days his job was to take one of the kids, usually Harry, and leave the house. Almost nothing in the outside world was open. There was little to see but he had fixed a child seat onto his bike, and he took Harry for bike rides each day. Golf courses were no longer permitted to operate so Paul rode to one with Harry to hunt for golf balls, much like an Easter egg hunt. Cafes were still serving takeaway, so sometimes they would grab a muffin or a croissant and sit on a park bench to eat it—in the dying months that Harry was still eating such things.

Something else strange had happened. Since the start of the second lockdown, Harry had quit wearing shoes all together. So now he went on bike rides with Paul in his socks. He would get out at a scenic spot and find himself unable to run around on the oval to chase magpies. He didn't like getting his socks wet, or anything else for that matter. It was winter. The grass was dew covered. It rained frequently. One drop of water on his clothes would send him into a meltdown. He obviously had severe sensory aversions. We carried two spare sets of clothes in his backpack at all times. Most days both would be used.

We attempted to let him run around on the pavement or gravel, but sticks, dust or soil sticking to his socks provoked the same response. We were at a complete loss. The one thing still permitted for Melbournians during the lockdown was to leave the house to exercise. Now Harry was unable to even do that! He also could not sit still at home, rolling around and thrashing constantly, although I couldn't tell whether it was due to excess energy or, as I was just starting to ponder, the need for some kind of sensory input.

I recall Paul coming home with Harry one day and both of them were in tears. He had attempted to take Harry on a train excursion to the city, something they hadn't done for a while. He had packed his shoes in his backpack and was convinced that at some point on the journey he would put them on. Instead, when they got out at the station in the city, Harry refused repeatedly and was on the verge of a meltdown. Paul had to carry him around everywhere as they walked through the city, now essentially a ghost town. By this point, Harry was almost fifteen kilograms. While he didn't eat much and was lean, we had kept up his baby formula and he had grown tall. Our bodies ached from the constant strain of picking up the kids, and that day Paul was spent from carrying Harry around the city for the past three hours. Harry didn't want a piggyback, nor would he sit up on the shoulders. He insisted on being carried around like a sack of potatoes and did very little to tension his body or grip on with his legs.

'Looking after Harry is like turning up to footy practice where everyone else has turned up to play footy,' said Paul, 'but Harry has turned up and he wants to play tennis and that's all he knows how to play.'

He was utterly defeated but he had summarised our misfit little boy perfectly. Paul was depressed. He spoke little and retreated to the bedroom at every possible opportunity to watch fly-fishing videos or buy bottles of whiskey to add to his growing collection. I was depressed by our home life and stressed with deadlines at work. News from all around the world was bleak. Death tolls from the virus were high around Europe and the United States. In the US, towards the end of August, the number of deaths was nearing 200,000. In Australia, that number was around 600 but infections were rising despite the oppressive measures. Both of us spent way too long following the terrifying yet addictive news—the virus was like a living beast, surging, feeding and morphing.

I wasn't afraid of catching COVID-19, but I was worried about global anarchy and how we were going to cope with being holed up indefinitely with Harry. Supermarket shelves were stripped bare. Panic-buying of toilet paper ensued, leading to a national shortage. People lost their jobs. Hours-long queues snaked outside Centrelink for welfare payments. Hospitals were at breaking point. Looting and violence no longer felt like fictitious scenarios. They felt just one step away from reality. We scrolled through Instagram late into the night, looking for images of a better life, only to find ourselves wide awake at 1.00 am. We drank whiskey, took sleeping tablets, then woke drowsily the next day to face another day much like the one before.

In the midst of all of this, Tessa was a little shot of espresso in our house. She had just started walking. This life was the only life she could remember, and she thought it was awesome. She was pushed and knocked, had toys snatched away, her bedroom ransacked. There was nothing to do. We had no visitors except Grandma who hadn't a clue how to play an age-appropriate game. Yet she woke from each nap with hazel eyes that were filled with wonder, her slightly upturned nose hinting at her playfulness. She was squeaky and chubby and bounced straight back up.

She wasn't afraid of Harry. She either forgave or forgot, but she was trouble. Repeatedly we separated them only to have her come running back to try to entice Harry into play again until, finally, she got hurt and came crawling to either Paul or me to seek comfort. Ten minutes later, she would be back at it again. Initially, she watched Harry's meltdowns and got upset, sometimes joining him in crying, other times offering comfort, bringing him toys or standing close. He misread her intentions and lashed out at her.

Being in extended lockdown meant there were times, usually on weekends when I wasn't working, that we had to take our daily outing as a family of four. Doing things as an entire family was something Paul and I dreaded, but there were simply not enough things to do to divide and conquer the entire day every day. One particular day, we decided to make use of the windy conditions to fly a kite at a sports field. Reluctantly, we rounded up the kids to put on their winter layers, and headed out the door, armed with multiple pairs of socks for Harry. Harry usually insisted on going out the door first, although sometimes he picked another order just to keep us on our toes, with the constant being that he dictated the order of procession.

On this day, he wanted Tessa to go out last, but we weren't to know that. I helped Tessa put her runners on and then I tentatively put a foot out the door and made eye contact with Harry who met my eyes and raised no objection. I proceeded without any issue. Tessa followed me. Harry screamed when he saw this and pointed to Paul. Then he pointed to Tessa now near the car and then back to Paul. Paul took Harry's hand and tried to pull him towards the door, but Harry held his ground. The order was wrong and now his screams were getting louder. I had an inkling there was an issue with the order of how we had exited the house. I kept my mouth shut. We had nowhere important to be. It seemed worthwhile to see how it would play out if we just pushed ahead. I was tired of pandering to Harry. Perhaps his meltdown would peak early and he would get over it.

I put Tessa in the car and buckled her up. Harry had been screaming for more than five minutes, frozen in the hallway near the door and still pointing at Tessa. Paul picked him up and carried him over to the car, exasperated. The meltdowns were averaging three a day and Paul had lost his usual chivalry. He opened the car door and put Harry into the seat. With one hand forcibly pressing him down, he used the other to pull out the straps and gestured for me to help him. I did so, reaching across Tessa while she gazed calmly at the agitated activity taking place next to her.

'Let's just drive,' said Paul.

We had never pushed through a meltdown before, but today we were both in the mood to try. Once Harry was clipped in, Paul got into the driver's seat as the meltdown continued, Harry purple in the face, stiff and braced in protest against the seatbelt. We backed out of the driveway and started heading for the oval. It wasn't subsiding. In fact, it was getting worse. We saw a police car, probably monitoring the lockdown orders, and somehow it felt inappropriate to continue past law enforcement with Harry in that state. Paul went around the block and pulled back into our driveway. I told Paul what I thought the problem was. He shrugged his shoulders with defeated indifference as we opened the car door and unbuckled the kids.

Tessa looked at us in confusion. She had been promised to fly a kite. She wasn't sure what that was, but knew it involved something more than simply driving a lap back to the house.

'We're just going to get out and go back in the house and try coming out again,' I tried to explain.

Paul unlocked the door and Harry bolted into the house and waited for the rest of us to join him, shuffling his feet on the spot impatiently but notably calmer now that he realised a remediation effort was under way. We all filed in and Tessa immediately turned around and tried to go back out. I held her back and improvised a playful hug, hoping she would not see the unfairness and pointlessness of this situation.

'Okay, Harry,' I said. 'Who goes out the door first?'

He pointed at Paul. Then he followed. Now outside the door, he pointed to me. Last of all came Tessa who did not like being left to the end and started to cry in protest. Now Tessa had tears rolling down her face, but it was just a little tantrum. A hug and a tickle from Paul resolved Tessa's grievance and soon she was squealing with laughter and squirming in his arms. Both kids got into their seats and were buckled in, and we drove off to the oval in silence save for a few dying sobs coming from Harry.

Tessa, Paul and I were living in captivity, hostages at the whim of a pint-sized madman. A sort of Stockholm syndrome. We loved our captor and did his bidding, structured our lives around him, even as it slowly destroyed us. One night when both kids were in bed, we sat down to drink whiskey and eat chocolate in front of the television.

'If we didn't have Tessa, I would not have ever known the joys of having a child,' Paul said to me.

I knew what he meant. We loved Harry fiercely, drove ourselves to exhaustion jumping through hoops to keep him happy, but we weren't getting much back. Until Tessa, we hadn't tasted the reciprocity of a normal parent-child experience.

THE STAIRCASE

Since Harry consumed the majority of his nutrition via his baby formula, his belly was constantly full of milk. He also seemed to have a strong gag reflex. Combined, these two factors resulted in a high number of incidents throughout infancy and toddlerhood where Harry would catch a cold, have a small coughing fit and regurgitate an entire bellyful of milk. For years during the winter months, we covered his fabric bedhead with towels and placed a rug next to his bed in an attempt to catch the vomit when he coughed at night. For an average cold, this could happen two or three times a night. The next morning, three sets of bedsheets would be piled up for the laundry. I frequently called on the services of a steam cleaner to sanitise and clean the carpets and couch, only to have to call the guy back two days later to go over the same areas again. I eventually decided to invest in a steam cleaner of my own.

Lockdown and social distancing saw the entire family spared of colds and flu for most of the winter season, but the kids caught one early on that was particularly memorable. Both Harry and Tessa had developed a mild cough. We took them separately for what was known as a PCR test, short for polymerase chain reaction test. In the first year of the pandemic, before the arrival of rapid antigen self-tests, anyone displaying symptoms was required to take a PCR test at one of a number of in-person or drive-through test centres. Contact tracers then went through the tedious task of identifying close contacts of the positive cases during their infectious period so that those people could take measures to isolate and prevent the further spread of the virus.

The process of a PCR test was unpalatable for most people, with a long nasal swab inserted high into each nostril and swirled around to obtain a sample. For an autistic kid with severe sensory aversions, this was akin to torture. Even before the actual test took place, one was already tormented by the act of lining up, in some cases for over an hour, at the peak of the virus. There were bizarre scenes of masked, sickly people standing in long queues, not quite the prescribed one and a half metres apart. Even if you didn't have COVID when you joined the queue, it seemed like a sure place to catch something while waiting for the test.

I ended up taking Harry to a drive-through test centre. I figured he would at least be restrained by the seatbelt. I drove there armed with colouring books for the wait and a pop-up lollypop as a reward at the end. I told him we were both going to take "a little test" since I had developed a sore throat, too. He didn't know what this was. It sounded cute. I explained to the nurse who came up to our window that this was likely to be difficult and she called a colleague for help. He and I pressed Harry's forehead and chest firmly against the seat, pinning him in place, while she swabbed his nose. Harry detested physical intervention at the best of times, and he announced this with a terrifying scream indicating that a grave violation of his bodily integrity had taken place. They attempted to obtain a sample from his other nostril, which was the usual protocol, but he put up such a fight they gave up. Their job was over in under a minute. I was left to deal with the fallout for the rest of the hour. I apologised to Harry profusely and cursed the pandemic and all its rules. I didn't intend to follow this one again.

The following night, Paul had just taken Harry out of the bath when he started coughing. Tessa had not yet washed her hair.

'Go find Mum,' Paul instructed, as he turned back to washing Tessa.

I was downstairs and heard Harry call out 'Mama' between coughs.

The Staircase

I raced up. He was halfway down the carpeted stairs when I met him. I had been drying the dishes and still had a tea towel in my hand. I reached him as he started to gag and held the tea towel up to his mouth, but I underestimated the volume of milk that was about to erupt. He had probably consumed 300 millilitres of milk over the past thirty minutes, an unknown quantity of apple juice, plus a small amount of chicken tender.

Instead of being a means to catch and absorb, the tea towel I was holding in front of him acted like a repellent shield. A fountain of vomit sprayed upwards and sideways. The spray smacked wildly and loudly against the walls in the manner of a hose turned up at high volume then partially obstructed by a thumb. He gagged again. Not having had sufficient time to process what had just taken place, I raised the tea towel and repeated exactly the same thing. This time, the vomit arched high up and rained straight down directly onto me standing a step lower than him, chunks of chicken landing in my hair. A third gag sent a heavy projectile directly onto my chest and down my tee-shirt, some of the contents settling in my bra. A final little spurt ended on Harry himself.

I stood unmoving, stunned. One part of my brain was telling me not to move to avoid spreading the sour stench that was dripping off me. Another other part of my brain was telling me I had no cleaning equipment within reach that I could use to contain the mess and therefore I had to move to acquire such equipment. Unfortunately, I had caught the same cold as Harry and had completely lost my voice earlier that day. I opened my mouth and screamed silently to Paul who was still in the bathroom with Tessa. The harder I tried to scream, the further down my throat my voice seemed to be pushed. Eventually, with the most minimal amount of effort I could muster to still emit a sound, I said in a quiet squeak, 'Help!'

Paul emerged from the bathroom and leaned casually over the staircase, completely unprepared for the scene below. He was still holding his phone and trying to watch a fly-fishing video.

'Oh my God ... What do you want me to do?' he stammered.

I couldn't speak, so shrugged unhelpfully. He began to shake with laughter. I was still frozen to the spot, thinking hard, wondering if there was a number I could call, a company perhaps, that provided a twenty-four-hour emergency cleaning service that would arrive with great urgency, sirens blaring, and race in to sanitise and deodorise our house because this was so far beyond an ordinary domestic situation. I eventually gave up on the idea, but only on account of the city being under lockdown orders.

I looked at this small human who stood on the steps in front of me. He was smiling, somewhat apologetically, somewhat proudly. Both his darling little dimples were sparkling.

'I did three vomits,' he announced. 'One in morning, one for lunch and one now.'

Then he pointed to his favourite pyjamas which were also covered in vomit and pulled at them, indicating he didn't like them dirty. He was incredibly cute. In a rare moment of compliance, he had done exactly what had been asked of him, to go and find Mum, but he had inadvertently created the kind of havoc that only Harry could create. The scene on the staircase was a fitting visual representation of life in lockdown with Harry, a living art.

Eventually, I undressed Harry and sent him back to Paul for a second bath. Then I began to undress myself. I took off my tee-shirt and my leggings which were covered in vomit that was slowly sliding down to the ground. I used my tee-shirt to scoop out the vomit from my bra then squashed the rest against myself. At least now it wasn't going to drip. Clad in only underwear, I was free to walk around the house without spreading further vomit to gather cleaning materials. I gestured to Paul and whisper-shouted a few instructions for him to commence the bedtime routine with both kids solo while I cleaned up the stairs.

For the next two hours, in bra and undies, I set about spraying and scrubbing the carpets with a bucket of soapy water. I saw no need to put on fresh clothes that were only going to be added to the overflowing pile of laundry. I wiped down the vomit off the walls, then steam cleaned the entire staircase. I stopped here and there to brush the kids' teeth. I stopped to sit with Harry while he did a poo, then left Paul to change him and put him to bed. Finally, at 10.30 pm, everything was as clean as it could possibly be under the circumstances, the kids were both asleep and I had showered. I logged onto my computer to begin my day's work.

THE DIAGNOSIS

'There are thirty-two steps required to get Harry through an average day,' Paul announced one evening.

He had calculated that from the time Harry woke to the time he went to bed, there were a minimum of thirty-two essential and unavoidable changes in activities or *transitions* we needed to get him to complete. With each one of them, Harry was locked in mortal combat with us. Getting out of bed involved continuous rounds of crawling around on the bed while he avoided his feet touching the floor until the time was just right. Getting dressed was met with refusal to wear anything other than blue clothing. Brushing teeth required us to follow him around the house and find opportunities to slide the toothbrush into his mouth. And changing nappies was to become a defining memory of lockdown number two.

Harry was not toilet trained until four years of age so he pooped in his nappy throughout the lockdowns. One of my most natural skills is the ability to observe and pick up on patterns, and this became my salvation in those early years with Harry. I had observed a pattern of behaviour that Harry displayed each time he was about to poop in the evenings. His bedtime was late, it was the second most challenging of the thirty-two transitions, and the negotiation to get him to bed usually took over an hour. At around 8.00 pm each night, we let him watch a children's video on the iPad while having a few corn puffs for supper. At some point, he would stand up and retreat to the corner of his bedroom or the walk-in robe and stand there or shuffle from one foot to another on the spot. Then he would gesture for Paul or me to come over. Sometimes he would want to hold our hand. Other times, he would want to fidget with a toy or brace against the doorframe. He always insisted on standing. He wanted the iPad to be held up for him at a certain angle and would adjust our hands that were holding the iPad to get it just right. Then, when everything was perfect, he would start to do his poo. Over time, I would prompt him to initiate this pattern by moving with the iPad over to the walk-in robe to help cue him that it was time to go, giving me a small ability to manage the time. If things went well, this would take a few minutes. Then the real challenge began.

I would get all the wipes and a fresh nappy and pull out the change mat. He had stopped voluntarily coming over once finished with his business, so I would approach him with the change mat. He invariably scuttled away. He would hide in one corner of the room, then run to another. Sometimes I would get him onto the mat only for him to roll off and escape again. If I chased him around too much, he got distressed. I normally called Paul for backup. Paul would come up and try to find something on the iPad sufficiently engaging that Harry would agree to lie down on the mat with the iPad held up above him while I changed his nappy. He was picky and got progressively more so as the lockdown wore on. I was not permitted to begin changing him until he had settled on something to watch. By August, we could no longer find any videos on the whole of YouTube that were good enough for Harry to agree to a nappy change. He started demanding Nana or Pa, meaning Paul's parents. He didn't understand why they were no longer coming to see him, so we resorted to video-calling them. It wasn't a guaranteed solution but, more often than not, it was just enough to get him to lay on the mat while they talked to him on the iPad.

By the end of July, the tension and panic in our household was rising much faster than the COVID-19 cases. Given the escalating severity of his behaviour, I requested one of his three psychologists continue seeing him face-to-face, which she thankfully agreed to, but all his other appointments moved online. Harry quickly learnt that the red button on the iPad screen was to hang-up a call, so all our online therapy sessions quickly became a series of ten short calls punctuated by Harry pressing the red button. During an appointment, the therapist sometimes wanted to engage directly with Harry. He would scuttle away or try to close the door behind him, and we crawled around the house following him with the iPad camera. Other times, the therapist wanted to speak directly with us to give us instructions or commentary about what had been observed, in which case Harry would come back deliberately to interfere with the conversation or hang up the call. He did not like to be discussed.

We persevered with these online appointments for most of the lockdown, largely due to a lack of any other alternatives and not being able to accept doing nothing as an option. Harry was simply too young and not sufficiently engaged in the therapy for it to be effectively delivered online. What he needed was hands-on, play-based therapy with access to novel toys and surroundings that he did not already have at home. It was a plight experienced by many in the disability community with younger children. Those with new diagnoses who did not already have established therapies in place were some of the worst affected by the move to online appointments. Over the two years that the lockdowns dragged across, thousands of children missed windows of opportunity for effective therapy, lost hard-earned gains or experienced costly delays in obtaining diagnoses.

In desperation, I rang clinic after clinic, hoping to find an occupational therapist who might be able to see Harry in person to assess his functionality, to view his disordered eating for themselves, to see firsthand his resistance to every one of his daily transitions. I pleaded with the receptionists taking my call to allow Harry to be seen under the lockdown exemptions due to his deteriorating function and the fact that no one would believe what I was describing unless they saw it with their own eyes. His defiance and resistance pervaded every moment of every aspect of his life, every task that we needed him to do, and even the ones that he himself wanted to do.

No one was accepting new clients, most certainly not in a face-to-face setting. Waiting lists for psychologists, paediatricians and other childhood specialists were so full many had closed their books. Most of the time, my calls went to an answering machine. My impatience was bubbling over. We were wasting precious time. Early intervention was the key to success for children like Harry. This had been stressed by our paediatricians, our liaison officers under the NDIS, in every piece of literature I had read about global developmental delay or autism. We needed to do real therapy with Harry right at that moment, not after the pandemic was over, whenever that was going to be. We were losing ground every day and I didn't have a clue how to halt it.

On 29 July 2020, when Harry was aged two years and six months old, we received his official diagnosis of Autism Spectrum Disorder—Level 2. Level 2, out of the possible three functional levels of autism, meant that he required "substantial support" according to the American Psychiatric Association's *Diagnostic and Statistical Manual of Mental Disorders, Fifth Edition*, or *DSM-5*, which is considered the authoritative guide for the diagnosis of autism in Australia.

For Paul, it was a bittersweet moment. He had for the past two years struggled to understand how he, someone who generally excelled at things, was so inept at parenthood, as if he had sat one exam after another and failed all of them. In the space of five minutes, one was easily capable of failing on multiple fronts in relation to Harry—failing to apply sunscreen, failing to get a hat on, failing to put shoes on, failing to get him into the car seat, failing to prevent him from squashing the petals of a flower he had just picked. Paul was unable to understand how his friends, some of whom had three, four, even five children, could manage to meet up for dinner at 7.00 pm while he, using best efforts, with me *and* a babysitter staying at home, could still only get there at 9.00 pm. The diagnosis excused Paul from what he had feared was a serious deficiency in his own skills.

For me, getting the diagnosis was like letting out a great sigh of relief. I had a name for it, a word other people recognised, that was legitimate in the medical community. It was a real disability, something I could use to both excuse his strange behaviour and force open doors for him. I had what I needed to put up a proper fight. It also finally gave me an explanation for the thing that had been troubling me the most. More than the anxiety or the meltdowns, it was the *unnaturalness* of everything he did that had made me so uneasy.

I told my friends about Harry's diagnosis the day I received it. I was so eager to give an explanation for his peculiar behaviour, to let them know that I didn't think it was okay, either. In his early years, there were so many times I wished I could have stuck a large, bright, orange label on him so that passers-by would understand he was autistic. It wasn't so much a problem when he had a meltdown, since when he was in the midst of one of those, he at least *looked* autistic, and the average bystander stood a good chance of recognising that. It was all those times when I was trying to avert the meltdown, when I was giving in to him and letting him get away with behaviour I would have frowned upon had I seen another parent do the same, that I wanted to explain. I was a harsh critic and I assumed everyone else was, too.

On 2 August 2020, the Victorian government declared a state of disaster, giving police powers to enforce restrictions on people's movements, and for the first time, Stage Four restrictions were introduced. The community transmissions had continued to rise under the Stage Three restrictions, with 760 mystery cases unable to be traced back to a source. The new restrictions provided the same four reasons for leaving the home, but now a five-kilometre radius limit was imposed. No one could go further than five kilometres from their home for the purposes of shopping or exercise. Exercise was limited to one hour outside per day and a curfew was in effect from 8.00 pm to 5.00 am. There was a border between metropolitan Melbourne and regional Victoria, where the virus had not yet taken hold. Face masks were mandatory outside the home. Things felt very grim.

This time, freshly armed with an autism diagnosis and subscribed to numerous autism and disability support groups, I had immediate access to information and interpretations on how to use the exemptions. Children with a disability were permitted to travel further than five kilometres for respite care at the home of a friend or relative, meaning we could take Harry to my parent's house, even though the respite was more for Harry than for me since, with his anxiety, I would need to stay with him the entire time. In-home care was permitted, and the carer was allowed to travel further than five kilometres to come to our home. Harry could also be taken for a drive further than five kilometres to manage complex behaviour. It was starting to dawn on me that lockdowns were going to be a way of life in 2020 and I needed to find a way to use all these exemptions.

Just as our relationship with Luna had started to unravel, we had for a few days used a fill-in nanny called Tessa, who we came to affectionately call Big Tessa. Her job for that first day was just to take care of little Tessa while I set Harry up with toys and tried to do a few minutes of work here and there. It would have been impossible for a newcomer to swoop in and just take over with Harry and we didn't bother attempting it, but Harry was curious about Big Tessa. Maybe it was because she was deliberately withheld from him, or because she was softly spoken, wholesome, with luxurious, long blonde hair that he had never seen before. Whatever it was, he followed the two Tessas to the door and watched them leave, cobbling a few words together to ask where they were going.

'Do you want to go to the park too?' I asked, already knowing the answer. 'You'll need to put your shoes on.'

He shook his head, but his eyes lingered and I saw the potential, so in August we enlisted Big Tessa to come around twice a week. I was wary that any more might result in burnout given the restrictive conditions she was working under, and I couldn't bear the thought of setting myself up for another Luna-style disappointment. It made an immediate difference in our lives to have Big Tessa. We were stuck in the house for most of each day, but we staggered the exercise outings to maximise the kids' time apart and bent the rules on the one-hour exercise limit. With Paul's help, Big Tessa managed to occupy the kids with Wiggles dance parties or sessions drawing with chalk or blowing bubbles out on the pavement.

Harry couldn't venture too far due to his lack of footwear. He was no longer happy with the pram, and I didn't expect Big Tessa to carry him around, but at least he was willing to step out of the front door with her or get in the car for drive-through hash browns. On a dry day, he was happy to wander up and down our street in his socks with Big Tessa, chasing magpies and looking for gumnuts until he inevitably stepped on something wet or spikey and wanted to come home. Importantly, it gave us a chance to spend some one-on-one time with little Tessa and treat her to rides in the shopping trolley on the one permitted supermarket trip each day.

On the weekends, to give Paul some time off from Harry, I began using the special exemptions to drive to my parents' house and unleash him there for an hour or two. He required my active presence the entire time, but it was at least a change of scenery, a different place where he could go to have a meltdown away from little Tessa. I purchased an inflatable pool and filled it with balls to make him a ball pit in their living room and he dove in and thrashed around. He had an obvious problem with staying still and there was at least some kind of sensory need being met in the ball pit that was satisfying for him. He laughed and smiled. He discovered the hilarious game of moving around Grandma's precious framed photos, re-arranging her ornaments, and hiding her phone. He would hide it and then demand to play with her phone to prompt her to begin a puzzled search for it. Similar fun was had with Grandpa's glasses. He was a disrupter, but he also had a sense of humour.

I had joined disability and autism forums on Facebook, and I asked how other parents in Melbourne were keeping their child's sensory needs met. Harry was destructive around the house. He never liked to build things. He liked to break them down, messily and forcefully. Lego and blocks were flung like projectiles around the house. One parent said there was a sensory play centre, purpose-built for children with disabilities, which was still operating on a single-family private hire basis. We were able to use our NDIS funding to book the entire facility for an hour and the whole household, including little Tessa, could go. We took the kids.

Tessa had little recollection of play centres before lockdown. This was the highlight of her life so far. She threw herself from one piece of equipment to another. A rocking horse, a basket swing, the trampoline, a climbing wall. Harry followed her around, dragging either Paul or me along. Tessa was the leader. She found each piece of equipment and knew intuitively how to play with it, or experimented until she worked it out. By contrast, Harry found a way to use everything in a manner other than that in which it was intended—he put his beloved Bun-Bun comforter on the rocking horse, he twisted the swing and watched it untwirl, he rolled around on the trampoline. He was fascinated by a small slide that had rollers which made the person going down it slide even faster. He watched as Tessa and then Paul and I went down it. We encouraged him. He put Bun-Bun on it to test it out. He made Paul put him on it and roll him down, holding his torso the entire time to prevent him from gathering momentum. Paul repeated the process five or six times until finally Harry was satisfied he had worked it out completely and climbed on to do it himself. He did it. He loved it and then he did it repeatedly and exclusively until the rest of the hour was up. I had just discovered two things about Harry. He was perfectionistic, and he was obsessive. He was forever observing and taking mental notes, but would not give anything a crack until he was satisfied he could do it with absolute perfection the first time. Then, if he liked it, he did nothing else but that.

Harry's speech was improving in great leaps and had significantly caught up on its initial delay. The speech therapy sessions continued to run online and were a source of extreme frustration for Paul who attended with him, but he put in an incredible amount of work with Harry outside of the sessions to practise what had been taught. Now even Big Tessa was able to have a meaningful, if disjointed, conversation with Harry. However, his speech and his relationship with Big Tessa were the two anomalies in his development that year.

As the lockdown wore on, Harry's challenging behaviour escalated in severity, especially his self-restricted diet. He had now stopped eating all fruit. The last to go were grapes. For a while he continued to eat black grapes and I exhausted all the supermarkets within a five-kilometre radius looking for them. I travelled further than five kilometres, carrying a copy of Harry's diagnosis with me in case I needed to explain to police why I needed to breach the travel limit to get black grapes. The lockdown led to food supply shortages. Eventually, items like imported grapes were not seen for the rest of the year. Harry had never eaten a vegetable in his life and with fruit struck off the menu his bowels bound up.

I tried to get an urgent appointment with a paediatrician to deal with Harry's nutrition, but it proved impossible. Even Harry's diagnosing paediatrician could only fit in an urgent telehealth appointment in several weeks' time. Paul didn't treat children in his practice, but as a doctor he nevertheless had the knowhow to start experimenting with different laxatives. We mixed some fibre supplement and an osmotic laxative into every bottle of milk. When things got bad, we used a stimulant laxative. When it had been several days, we used a suppository. The most compliant of children would have recoiled at the first sign of a suppository. Giving one to Harry was as traumatic for us as it was for him. The first time we tried one was soon after Big Tessa started working with us, and after five days of straining and waiting for an elusive bowel action. She saw the whole thing. Us pinning him down against his will on his tummy, him fighting back and screaming until he gagged. To top it off, when Harry realised what we were planning to do he had insisted, in a final act of defiance, that this be carried out in the backyard so our entire neighbourhood could hear what went down. She was so shaken by it we wondered if she would ever come back.

Some nights, Harry stood in his corner of the walk-in robe and strained until his face went purple for forty-five minutes, even an hour. Bedtimes frequently blew out past 10.30 pm and on those nights, his eyelids were drooping while he strained to poop. The whole time, he needed us to sit right near him and hold his hand and the iPad. It was heartbreaking work.

Soon we had another problem. Harry had been eating only chicken tenders for dinner every night, a pattern that is still ongoing today. He screamed and sometimes ran away if another item appeared next to the chicken tender on his plate, even without any expectation that he eat it. The pandemic supply shortages were affecting our ability to get hold of the two brands of chicken tender he was willing to eat. One brand was sold at each of the major supermarket chains, and I am convinced they came out of the same factory and were simply branded differently. Harry was the ultimate blind taster and he accepted both but rejected all others. Since they came from the same factory, both ran low on stock at the same time. I tried other chicken tenders. 'Too light', 'too small' or 'broken' for crumbing that had a tendency to fall off. Harry had also developed a habit of not eating the part of the food he was holding, so he ate two-thirds of the way down the tender and considered the last part inedible.

I logged onto the computer to check stock levels at different supermarket locations, hunting down the last few boxes of this precious chicken tender around Melbourne. I drove way past the five-kilometre radius to gather them. In the carparks of the supermarkets, I got the closest I had ever been to a religious experience—I prayed, hands clasped, that there would be a box of the correct chicken tenders in the freezer. Entering supermarkets filled me with an anxiety I had never known. I wandered up and down the aisles teary and feeling utterly desolate, wanting to find these chicken tenders, yet also afraid to look for them lest I find an empty shelf, convinced I was the only parent in the world ever to go through this. I desperately scanned the shelves, looking for that one brand of rice cakes or the one flavour of corn puffs Harry ate.

Paul and I continued to argue about how to deal with Harry's eating. He thought I was going about it the wrong way, but wasn't able to come up with another way and admitted that doing nothing was also not an option. We both agreed it was a real possibility that Harry might stop eating solids all together and revert exclusively to drinking from a bottle like a baby. At two and a half, he was still tall for his age but thin. His spine protruded sharply from his back. He had reduced his food intake to two packets of eight-gram corn puffs a day, half a chicken tender and sometimes a rice cake or the outer rim of a McDonald's hash brown. The remainder of the time, he subsisted on his baby bottle. Bizarrely, he did not seem to ever get a hunger cue.

Seeing his dependence on the bottle, we tried moving the milk into a sippy cup or a straw cup, hoping for him to at least use an age-appropriate drinking container. He adamantly refused and insisted it tasted different. I demonstrated making the milk and pouring it into his bottle, then from his bottle into the sippy cup. He saw it and understood, but was unable to overcome his sheer inflexibility. He demanded the bottle when he was upset or hungry, and even after drinking the last drop, he continued sucking on the empty bottle or gnawing on it for comfort.

We finally got an appointment with his paediatrician. She had been in high demand. Children on the autism spectrum or with other disabilities had been disproportionately and severely affected by the lockdown. Therapies and services had been limited or cut, established routines disappeared, people wore strange masks and the places they normally frequented to meet sensory self-soothing needs—rocking or swinging at the playgrounds—were closed. Amaze, the peak support group for autistic individuals and their families in Victoria, conducted a survey across August and September of families with school-age autistic children and around seventy per cent of families reported deteriorating mental health and wellbeing. We were not alone in our suffering, but with a brand-new diagnosis, we did not have any autism-specific service providers, and none of them were commencing new intakes at this time.

'His diagnosis of ASD 2 means he needs substantial support,' I said despairingly to the paediatrician. 'But I think if you were assessing him now, he's worse than that. It's like he needs someone to fully execute every daily function for him, but he also fights that support.'

She nodded sympathetically.

'Yes, we do give them a rating on the spectrum and expect that to last a lifetime, but in fact, kids change and at different times, they are better or worse. It's possible that assessed right now, he could qualify as ASD 3.'

In practical terms, it didn't matter. Even if he were ASD 3 and eligible for more funding and more supports, there was no way to even use any of that for the moment.

I asked about a feeding tube which was sometimes given to children with ARFID, but she thought Harry's opposition to any kind of physical intervention made that an untenable option. Now that we had a diagnosis in hand, she suggested we try a children's meal replacement formula and wait until the end of lockdown to get him into a feeding program run by a specialist autism centre she was willing to make an urgent placement request for. The meal replacement would contain a far greater calorie content than his regular baby formula and had a complete range of essential nutrients needed for his stage of development. It could be given in his bottle in place of his regular formula since that was the most efficient delivery system. She didn't think now was the right time to be weaning him off the bottle.

That first day I brought home the purple tub of meal replacement formula, Harry saw it and asked in alarm what had happened to his milk which came in a blue tub of the same size and shape.

'I don't like purple milk,' he cried in distress.

Underneath all his anxiety, I had long recognised in Harry a real sharpness of mind. He had an excellent awareness of his surroundings. Nothing that was new or out of place was lost on him. I don't recall Harry ever losing his toys. I wouldn't realise how remarkable that was until Tessa became a toddler and was forever crying about her misplaced toys.

'The purple milk is for me,' I lied.

From that point onwards, he took his bottle from me with great suspicion. He asked to make his own milk and pulled a step ladder across when it was time to prepare one. I became an illusionist at the kitchen bench. I used decoys and developed skills in clandestine manoeuvres, switching and hiding bottles behind tubs and jars, simultaneously pointing out a fly in the house that we never seemed able to get rid of. I was forced to mix small amounts of the meal replacement formula into his bottle of baby formula and gradually increase it over six months before he was fully converted. Anytime I tried to progress a little faster he would hand the bottle back to me declaring, 'It's purple milk, I don't like it!' He obviously saw through the deception at some stage in the process, although he was willing to humour me so long as he saw I was working hard to keep the deception alive.

The effort of keeping Harry sustained with sufficient nourishment preoccupied all my waking hours and festered as uneasy dreams in my tortured sleep. I came to have only negative associations with food, not just in relation to Harry, but also for myself. Eating had become a traumatic daily undertaking. There were lots of things to dread about the day, but the one I dreaded the most was dinner and the recurring question of what to cook for it. For Harry, that answer was easy. But Paul was coeliac and Tessa, having watched Harry's highly abnormal feeding patterns, had become picky as well. For me, nothing was appealing anymore. Dinners rolled around too frequently, a chore to get out of the way each day. It was forty-five minutes where I had to sit and watch a constant stream of self-sabotage and non-functional behaviour. The fact that Harry was on a nutritionally complete meal replacement didn't dull the grating sight of what played out at the dinner table each night. I found no pleasure in eating even my favourite meals. I forced food into my mouth at mealtimes to model appropriate behaviour, but my body no longer reminded me to eat. Perhaps this was what eating felt like to Harry.

PATHOLOGICAL DEMAND AVOIDANCE

One of the psychologists who treated Harry practised a style of therapy known as Theraplay®, a play-based psychotherapy for children. Aside from his restrictive eating, our key frustration with Harry was his difficulty with transitions, commonly referred to as non-compliance. Vanessa set out a large number of colourful balloons and said to Harry, 'Can you tap the red ones?' Harry proceeded to touch all of them except for the red ones. He knew red. He understood the request. He was hard-wired to resist.

She changed tack. She began throwing balloons into the air randomly and Harry was immediately motivated to hit the ones flying through the air. He touched a red one.

'Great work getting the red one, Harry,' she cried enthusiastically, hoping the reinforcement of being praised for hitting the right one would motivate him to comply.

He grumbled in protest. He shunned the praise and hid behind me while continuing to vocalise his discontent.

Vanessa had accepted Harry as one of the few clients she was still seeing face-to-face, even though he refused to enter the room until she had removed her facemask. She could see that, language aside, he was losing function the further the lockdown wore on. He began turning up to the appointments in his pyjamas and socks after refusing to get dressed into day clothes or to wear shoes. His hair was tangled and needed to be cut but he wouldn't let me. It needed to be washed more than once every two weeks, but he had a severe aversion to getting his hair wet and there was no way to wash it other than with one adult pinning him against the side of the bathtub while the other doused him. We were traumatised by what we were doing and couldn't bring ourselves to do it more frequently.

Vanessa worked in a clinic that was continuing to run in-person appointments for its most severely affected clients. I begged her to help me find an occupational therapist. OT was the last of the mainstream treatment modalities that we hadn't tried. I didn't really understand the discipline, but I wasn't able to rest until I at least had put Harry in front of an OT. Vanessa had seen Harry thrashing and writhing around on the floor in her sessions. She thought he was seeking sensory input which an OT could help to interpret. She was concerned enough to make a request to the OT working next door to see Harry in person, jumping extensive waiting lists. At the very least, he could use some of the sensory play equipment in there.

We were turning up to that therapy centre twice a week. Often, I parked and was unable to coax him out of the car. He refused to get out of his seat or step out of the car, claiming 'my legs are tired'. He procrastinated and climbed into the driver's seat and pretended to drive. I began arriving half an hour early to make sure we got in on time. On many days, we were still late. I had the reverse problem when we tried to leave. He refused to get into the car seat. I tried asking. I tried instructing. I tried forcing. Each tactic was futile. He was almost seventeen kilograms and tall. I was forty-eight kilograms. Although I had a light build, I was usually strong. But that year, I had deconditioned from not climbing and had overuse injuries from handling two small children. My wrists and thumbs hurt from wrangling him. I hid all sorts of surprises in my handbag to use as bribes to get him into the car seat—a party blower, some stickers, a finger puppet, some collectable action figures. These would all work, but only once, and I had to keep stocked with new items. I passionately hated knickknacks. We lived in a waste-conscious household and both kids had used washable nappies and wipes until they turned one. I had spent years at supermarket checkouts glaring my disgust at parents who took the plastic collectable knickknacks. Now I couldn't get my hands on them fast enough. I was buying them from other people on eBay to get the full sets for Harry.

Eventually, Vanessa asked if we had heard of "PDA". I had not. Pathological Demand Avoidance. In the UK, this is recognised as a sub-type of autism and can be included as part of the diagnosis. For example, one could say "Harry has a diagnosis of ASD2 with a PDA profile". However, PDA is not recognised under the DSM-5. In Australia, it is not officially recognised and is still little known among professionals. Despite his autism diagnosis, we were still extremely baffled. Autism seemed to only partially explain the quandary that was Harry—his inflexibility and rigidity. All else remained a diabolical mystery, nothing that standard literature on autism thematically alluded to, let alone offered an explanation for.

PDA was originally described in the early 1980s by a UK psychologist, Elizabeth Newson, as a syndrome in which a person exhibited extreme resistance to, and avoidance of, the ordinary demands of life, even when compliance was in that person's best interest. Such demands included each of the thirty-two transitions Paul and I were struggling to get Harry through each day. A demand could also be as simple as having to answer a question from someone, the physiological need to eat or the latent expectation to say "hello". For years, Harry refused to use the word *hello* in context. He deliberately substituted it with *goodbye*. If he was feeling particularly cooperative, he would hold up his favourite toy, Bun-Bun, and put on a cute bunny voice to squeak out a 'hello' then immediately add for clarification, in his own voice this time, 'That was Bun-Bun talking, okay?'

Paul frequently described Harry as a contrarian. If only it were as quaint as that sounded! One of Harry's psychologists thought he was potentially exhibiting oppositional defiance disorder, but he lacked the necessary hostility for it to be a satisfying explanation. Sometimes he was angry or combative, but most often he seemed either distressed about a demand, or devious in the way he evaded it. This, along with a list of some twenty other distinguishing features, were the hallmarks of PDA, and upon discovering them, it was the first time I realised there possibly existed an entire *type* of people out there who were just like Harry.

Recent studies have refined descriptions of PDA, frequently referencing it as an anxiety-based need for control or autonomy. Faced with a demand, even one that the person may have placed upon themselves and want to meet, something desirable such as going on a holiday, they are unable to meet it due to the anxiety produced by the expectation of meeting it. Demands may be avoided by the use of distraction or manipulation, or by the child attempting to take control. Often such children are more comfortable with following demands when in role play. A unique feature that children with PDA frequently exhibit is a delay in language followed by an explosive catch-up phase which especially caught my attention since that was exactly what had happened with Harry.

PDA was complicated. It seemed far more nuanced and placed the parent in a significantly less influential position than "classic" ASD. While many children with autism display a reluctance to follow demands, they generally do so by employing a non-social approach, such as by ignoring or shutting themselves off. PDAers, on the other hand, possessed what Newson described as "surface sociability". They had an ability to superficially manage social interactions, for example, with normal eye contact and good conversational skills, but lacked a deeper understanding of social responsibilities, boundaries and social identity, with PDA children often seeing themselves as equals with adults. Alarmingly, I read that strategies which normally worked with ASD children such as consistency, routine and repetition were usually ineffective for children with a PDA profile.

PDA children responded better to novelty and low-demand environments, having an adult fulfil demands with them collaboratively, rather than being directed or requested by them to do something. The affliction sounded ridiculous, more like a calculating power play than a disability, yet it described the toddler dominating our house so accurately. Was I being hoodwinked by one outrageous and elaborate excuse to get away with being a pain in the arse?

Harry's desire to control everyone in our household was a source of elemental torment to me. Seven years earlier, I had been briefly married to an overtly controlling and covertly anxious man. Here I was again, in a domestic relationship subjected to control by a controller playing the vulnerability card, but this time I couldn't just pack my bags and leave. I despised it, hated it, felt degraded each time I indulged it.

I spent hours on online forums reading about PDA. I was astute enough to know that much of the advice proffered around on the forums was of questionable or speculative quality. Generally, the parents on there had one PDA child which made them as much of an expert on PDA as me, but we were bonded in a shared kind of torture, and there was little professional content about PDA available. It became a self-perpetuating spiral of depression. I was lost and needed to hear stories about other people in my shoes. So, I read them and I related—everyone on there was so desperate. Some had children who were physically violent or self-harming, whom they had to call the police on. Others were isolated or unemployed as their child refused to go to school or leave the home, so they couldn't either. Many were from single-parent households. Some were couples contemplating separation because the stress and differences of approach in raising their child had placed such an intolerable strain on their relationship.

Traditional schooling seemed to be a universal failure among PDA children, with some seventy per cent either refusing school, being home schooled or "unschooled" and many of those still attending school doing so with modified arrangements. The forums were filled with discussion on "school can't" which PDA advocates describe as a situation where a child is not refusing to go to school, nor are they choosing not to, they simply *can't*. The education system was heavily criticised across the forums for not being progressive enough to meet the needs of PDA kids by providing accessible alternatives to the traditional schooling model.

I started worst-case scenario planning. I could totally see this happening with Harry. He couldn't even leave the house with grandparents. How on earth would he ever go to school or kindergarten? What would he eat for lunch there? Was I going to have to homeschool him for his entire educational life? If he didn't go to school, then how would he ever get a job? If he was going to live at home forever, was he going to be like this forever? He was the son of a doctor and a lawyer. He had to go to school!

In those early days of discovering PDA, when I bathed in the dark comfort of this shared experience, I also found myself straddling an uncomfortable dichotomy. PDA support groups overwhelmingly favoured a low-demand lifestyle and so-called radical acceptance of the neurodiversity. Late at night when I closed my laptop after hours of trawling through posts and comments, I was left with the echoes of parents' pleas for understanding from the education system, the healthcare system, their friends and families, to be more accommodating to this unique group of children who were hampered by an invisible but debilitating disability. But the world was made to suit the able masses and as someone who valued efficiency so highly, I understood why.

Until that point in life, I thought I was endowed with a pretty good conscience. I thought I embraced tolerance as a virtue and diversity as a value, but the full extent of Harry's disability had just hit me. Up until then, *disability* had been a handy label I could use to have an in-home carer during lockdown, but now I felt the full weight of the word. I may have looked with charitable compassion at someone else raising a disabled child, viewed that person as conducting parenthood with greater honour than the rest of us, but it was an entirely different matter to be saddled with a disabled child of my own. There was no escaping this shameful truth I had just discovered about myself. What I truly believed, in that most secretive and murky place where beliefs lie, was that disabled lives were worth less. I was tortured and unable to reconcile the fierce love I *felt* for Harry with what I really *thought* of him. I was the ableist who found herself pleading a compassionate case for the special treatment of her autistic son.

THE WAR IN MY MIND

I was supposed to be working from home. Instead, I had just taken Harry to the occupational therapist and was deep in negotiations with him to get into the car seat so that I could get home in time for a meeting. He procrastinated. He sat in the driver's seat and turned the steering wheel, adjusted the mirrors, the tilt of the seat. Then he crawled into the footwell to inspect the pedals and the railing that adjusted the amount of legroom. Some thirty minutes elapsed and suddenly he stood up and braced against the seat. He was doing a poo. Sometimes a poo happened during the day, and I was grateful for it whenever it took place. Another fifteen minutes to complete that. Now the real challenge, I had to do the nappy change in the back of the car.

I pulled out the nappy change bag. He scrambled around the car as I tried to round him up, protesting that he wasn't finished, but I knew from the amount of movement that he was done. I pleaded, begged, cried. We had been in the carpark an hour and my call was in fifteen minutes. Finally, I found a four-coloured pen in the car. He hadn't seen one before and it was enough to keep him occupied while I changed his nappy. Once changed and clipped into his car seat, I drove off. It was close to lunchtime, and I handed a yoghurt pouch to Harry as I drove. He had become unreliable with these lately and I knew before long yoghurt would be dropped too. I watched him anxiously in the rear-vision mirror to see if he would take it. He was fiddling with the yoghurt lid in one hand and about to have some when the lid fell and rolled under the seat in front.

'Lid, lid! Mama, get the lid!' he cried.

I was moving in seventy-kilometre-per-hour traffic. It was not possible for me to reach around under the seat.

'Just wait till we stop at the red light,' I said to him.

'Now! Now! Get the lid now! I can't have the yoghurt. I never want yoghurt again!'

I watched Harry in the rear vision mirror straining against his seatbelt, legs stiffened and back arched as he tried to burst out of his seat. He had squeezed the open yoghurt pouch in his clenched hand so that yoghurt was now on his pants. Utterly stricken with distress, his upper torso was trying to break free from his legs and that terrifying patch of yoghurt, the way one might behave if it had been an enormous spider.

'Clean it up! Clean it up! Get the lid! Mama, do it now!' he screamed.

Suddenly, I was overcome with uncontainable emotions. In the moment that I realised they were about to overwhelm me, I chose not to fight back. I turned to face them eyes wide open and beckoned them come eat me alive. I pulled over on the side of the road and switched off the engine. I unclipped my seatbelt and turned my whole body around in the seat to face Harry. I had the biggest meltdown of my life.

'You are an intolerable, pathetic little shit!' I yelled at his face with such force my voice cracked and broke. Hot tears rolled. 'I cannot believe I am stuck with you for the rest of my life! Why can't you just be normal? What is wrong with your brain!'

I had completely lost control. I was suddenly energised and empowered by my own rage. My emotions had been spring loaded for months. Now they were out and lashed around wildly, inexorably. I felt might and vigour I hadn't felt before, and strangely I didn't want this ugly tirade to stop. I ranted, spraying expletives and other curses I hope Harry was too young to remember. He was no longer screaming but sobbing quietly, watching me in the same stunned silence I had watched him countless times before.

Three minutes later, I was done. The demon had been excised for now. I picked up the yoghurt lid and cleaned up the yoghurt on Harry.

'I'm sorry, I shouldn't have done that. That was wrong. Mama's sorry,' I said, searching his face for any signs of damage from what he had just witnessed.

'Can I have the four-colour pen again?' he asked.

He still had his post-meltdown hiccups, but he had zeroed in on something new. His visible emotional range was limited like that. Whatever he was processing – fear, shock, confusion – was concealed within the walls of a peaceful but inexpressive face. I found the pen, got back into the driver's seat and started the engine. I played Wiggles songs as the two of us headed back home, as if I hadn't just committed a major violation of the parenting code of conduct.

By now it was the end of August and Melbourne had been locked down for close to two months, with Stage Four restrictions for a full month. The business of living was unbearable and there was no end in sight as community transmissions of the virus remained high. Depression hung over the entire city of Melbourne, materialising as dripping, grey winter clouds.

Tessa pointed hopefully to the taped-off playgrounds as she wandered around in a raincoat and gumboots, splashing in puddles on her one-hour exercise outing. Melbournians were enduring a way of living that was to have social repercussions for an entire cohort of young children in the years to come. Everyone was required to wear face masks. There were no signs of a friendly face. Tessa tried to approach other children on her daily walks, offering gumnuts and friendship. She longed to play and touch, but now the awkwardly polite thing to do was to steer one's child away in the practice of social distancing, to keep the requisite one and a half metres apart from the next person.

At the beginning of the second lockdown, I had yearned to go climbing and worried about losing my grip strength and conditioning.

I missed the strenuous but graceful movement which satisfied some deep need for a primal expression. In July, I had ordered a finger board which I installed above a doorway and would do a few pull-ups or lock-offs each time I passed beneath it. Two months later, it hung in disuse. I ducked my head in avoidance as I walked under it and looked at it as if it were a relic from another era. I couldn't even be bothered to take it off. I had lost the will to live.

Paul and I didn't speak anymore unless it was in relation to household chores or the management of the children. I was either holed up in the study working while he was occupying the kids, or I had taken over caring for the kids to allow him to hide in the bedroom, most likely watching fly-fishing videos. He had become a housemate and a workmate. We were living and working under the tyrannical rule of a two-and-half-year-old. Harry's bedtime defiance and toileting routine sometimes stretched to 10.30 pm, and it resulted in us setting up one bedroom for him upstairs and another downstairs for Tessa, to give her the best chance possible at following a normal toddler routine. So, Paul and I slept in separate beds on separate floors of the house to attend to the needs of each child during the night. Occasionally, one of us attempted a sleepover in the other's room, only to sneak out in the wee hours of the morning to return to the comfort of their own bed.

What started as a temporary measure to ensure adequate sleep for all of us had become a standing arrangement. The spare bedroom was somewhere I could go at the end of a long day to break up one long day from the next long day, somewhere to let my stony-faced guard down and know that nobody could see me cry. I began to view it as a sort of sanctum, although I found no true peace there either. I was exhausted during the day but agitatedly awake at night, my mind alive with disjointed chatter. I passed the torturous hours on a rotating combination of melatonin, sleeping pills and herbal sleep aids.

Perhaps I could ask my father to get rid of Harry for me. I was having vivid and extreme fantasies about what to do with the Harry problem. My dad was eighty-five at the time, stoic, useful and practical. Whenever I visualise my dad, I see him as a dependable figure in the background, unspeaking and almost unmoving, silhouetted because I've never really known him in detail, but he has always been there whenever I needed him. He loved me and I loved him in a detached and distant way.

I have never experienced any kind of meaningful emotional attachment with either of my parents, nor them with each other as far as I can tell. They are still married but probably should have divorced some thirty years ago. They no longer even fight and to this day, I have never heard them say the words "I love you" to one another. If I heard that now, forty years too late, I would squirm with discomfort. Yet I have never doubted their love for me. Everything they have done in their lives has been with the intent of making mine better. In my mother's case, she pursued this so doggedly and immutably, with the kind of suffocating vehemence and complete disregard to my autonomy and dignity, that it has emotionally repelled me from her since my teens.

Still, in my moment of need, when I was consumed entirely by hopelessness, my thoughts went straight to my parents to help me, as if I were still a little girl. As one final gesture of love to me, I thought my dad, given his advanced years, would not mind taking Harry for a drive and crashing the car straight into a tree. I had retreated to bed early to indulge in these thoughts. But what if I asked my dad to do this and he refused? Would he tell Paul and derail my entire plan?

What I really wanted was to protect Tessa, that soft, giggling marshmallow of a toddler who evoked all the motherly instincts I didn't know I had. I looked at her strong little thighs that kicked her feet around gleefully, her stocky barrel-like body, her perfect, light, golden skin. I devoured her with my eyes, squeezed her in my arms. She was a robust little thing and squealed with delight at my hearty hugs. I felt protests of unfairness swell within me each time I saw her pushed and scratched by Harry, knowing full well if I gave him the reprimand he deserved, it would pave the way for a meltdown that would consume the next hour of my time, so I rarely did. He was allowed to get away with it most of the time, and the injustice I felt for Tessa burned intensely. I didn't want her to be intimidated by Harry's sustained high-octane meltdowns. I worried what witnessing Harry's behaviour was doing to her developing little brain. What would happen to her when Harry was fifteen years old and wanted something she had? If his two-year-old behaviour had been taking place from a teenage body, he would have been behind bars.

My catastrophising was now blaring full blast. I desperately wanted to save my daughter from the life my son was condemning all of us to. I wanted to give her a happy and normal life, the chance to live in a safe and peaceful home, for her to one day be able to do homework in peace without her brother raging outside her door, to have parents, or at least one parent, who could make her a priority. I didn't want to think she would spend the best years of her life tagging along or cast aside to babysitters, a thing to be dealt with while we took Harry from one appointment to another.

I wanted to tell her that in the short time I had been her mother she had filled me with a delight I had never known. I had experienced the warmth of seeing all my giving returned to me in the form of little hands that cradled my face or clumsily stroked my hair. Her hazel eyes sought mine. Her gentle smiles were offered to me not because I was holding a toy that she wanted, but as an invitation to connect my world with hers. She gave back. Her emotional register was full. The words of Zora Neale Hurston plagued my mind daily: *I have been in Sorrow's kitchen and licked out all the pots*. Anything that resembled liveliness had turned to decay. I was like salmon that had swum upstream only to spawn and die, yet I took one look at Tessa and felt that my life hadn't all been a waste.

I began to fantasise about other options. Perhaps I could say I was taking Harry hiking. I knew of some cliffs I liked to climb that were vantage points on hiking tracks. I could place Harry in the child-carrier backpack, walk up one of those tracks and take him in my arms for a closer look over the edge.

I visualised in magnificently high detail, in vibrant colour. Pale blue skies, a thin veneer of mist burning off in the sun, eucalyptus leaves stirring in the breeze. I had Harry pressed tightly against me, chest to chest, his face looking out over my shoulder. I chatted in tender motherly words to him. 'Can you hear the birdies?' I asked softly. In my mind, I could hear my breath as I lifted my feet high to clear chunky boulders. Sticks crunched beneath the soles of my boots. I felt the sunlight on my skin and Harry's weight in my arms. I stood on the edge calmly, our last moments together. I had brought my little boy to see my paradise. I felt us falling into dead air as my feet pushed powerfully away from the cliff. It was a muted sort of effort, immediately converted downwards into gravity, a feeling I remembered well from skydiving. In the air, we began to rotate so that our heads tipped downwards first. I heard Harry start to cry and felt an immediate pang of doubt. A blur of leaves and branches. Glimpses of blue sky. I looked down to meet the ground rush.

Slowly, I would come to witness us in the third person, the crumpled mess of a mother and her child, a gruesome scene softened by dappled sunlight through tall trees and birdsong still chiming in the background. With the drama over, I would return to my reality, lying there alone in my bed feeling a deep, sad, aching love for my little boy whose mind was sealed firmly shut from me.

How close was I to acting upon this? Probably not that close, but I had become obsessed and infatuated with my nightly ritual of visualising it. It was as if by creating this highly detailed and believable scenario where I could remove my son and myself from the world, I was comforted by the knowledge that there was a viable escape, should I need it. Each time I jumped off this cliff, it set in motion a sort of climactic arousal of deranged emotions. Its completion somehow calmed me enough so I could carry on in real life.

FINDING A WAY FORWARD

I continued to languish in my state of depression, but there was nothing that could be done about it. I revealed little to Paul about my darkest thoughts, but he knew from my outbursts of rage at a spoon falling off the table or water splashed out of the bathtub that I was at breaking point. He suggested I speak to the GP about taking antidepressants to survive the rest of the lockdown. He had been tiptoeing around Harry and now he was tiptoeing around me. I had no time to see a psychologist, I was up to my eyeballs with appointments for Harry. I reached the conclusion that every parent of a special needs child arrives at by default: the luxury of a proper solution for myself would have to wait. I spoke to my GP over the phone and completed a questionnaire. I was suffering from an adjustment disorder, she said. I wondered how many times a day she was giving out that diagnosis. She agreed to prescribe Zoloft. I could never tell if it helped or not, which probably means it didn't, but I took it anyway.

We had now made it to September. The Stage Four restrictions were originally scheduled to end in the middle of the month. Instead, Victoria's premier Daniel Andrews apologetically announced it had been extended to the end of the month with some minor adjustments to the curfew, an extension from one to two hours of daily exercise and the introduction of a "singles bubble" so that Victorians living alone could choose one friend to create a social bubble with.

Meanwhile, my climbing partner, Jo, had become one of a sizeable proportion of Victorian women who had curiously developed a crush on the state's Chief Health Officer, Dr Brett Sutton. He featured daily at the press conferences alongside Andrews, providing information on the virus and explanations about the health directions. Fed on a diet of lockdowns and rolling COVID-19 news, everyone was bored and losing their minds. Admittedly, if you stared at Sutton long enough, he did eventually start to take on a faint likeness to Kevin Costner. Jo started sending daily memes. Here was Brett Sutton's head superimposed onto James Bond's body for the promotional poster of *Die Another Day*. And here was Brett Sutton dressed as naughty Santa because it was the start of September and everyone was wishing their lives away until the end of December. It was a welcome slice of comedy in my day.

We had just stopped seeing Vanessa. She had expected the effects of Theraplay® to be evident by now if it was to be an effective therapy. She had tried valiantly, but this psychologist now felt unscrupulous in continuing with a therapy she no longer believed would yield results. She didn't know what else to do for Harry.

'Pick your battles and just prioritise his health and safety for the moment,' she advised. 'Everything else can wait until lockdown is over and you can see what is available on the other side.'

Our other psychologist had moved to another state, and in any case, I had long concluded that one hour of psychology each week was not making a dint in Harry's behaviour. We continued with occupational therapy since it at least gave him access to a gym setting similar to a play centre, but my thoughts were the same. One hour once a week amounted to zero gain there, too. I rang a friend, Debbie, who was an educational psychologist working in schools with kids who had learning and behavioural challenges.

'Have you heard of PDA?' I asked her. 'Do PDA kids manage to go to kinder?'

Harry was eligible for kinder the following year, although even in the best-case scenario, we were always going to hold him back until the one after. Still, kinder and schooling preoccupied my thoughts. Any hope of getting him there would require preparatory work years in advance.

She hadn't heard of PDA, but when I described it, her response was to direct me to focus on the autism diagnosis rather than the PDA profile.

'Many of the presentations of PDA are common in children with autism and children with other diagnoses,' she said. 'Forget the label. Look at the specific behaviours and how to understand and manage them.'

It was to be a rhetoric we heard time and again from nearly all of Harry's treating professionals. The majority of Australian autism experts did not recognise PDA. Initially, I felt dismissed. This thing was real. How could we treat it if no one believed in it? Over the course of the next few years, I eventually came to see that the non-recognition of PDA as its own distinct profile did not necessarily prevent us from finding successful treatment or strategies. But at the time, it felt like we were predestined to fail. Debbie recommended we engage a board-certified behaviour analyst, otherwise known as a BCBA, to analyse Harry's functional behaviour.

I researched BCBAs. They all seemed to be linked to something called ABA therapy. I was getting lost with all the letters. There weren't many BCBAs in Melbourne. The pathway to becoming one seemed arduous and difficult, involving a master's degree in applied behaviour analysis, 1,500 hours of field work and passing a certification exam. I found the names of about ten BCBAs and rang all of them. All their waiting lists were full, or the therapy centres were not taking any new clients during lockdown. One centre that called me back was Happy Oak Behavioural Consulting, and I received a call from Tineke, the BCBA herself. She heard Harry screaming in the background demanding I get off the phone. It was the foreground, really. He had climbed up my leg and was hanging off my arm, pulling the phone down towards him. He was controlling whenever I took phone calls.

Tineke's centre wasn't taking new clients during lockdown either, although as a disability service they were continuing face-to-face services for existing clients. She offered to schedule an online intake meeting for the following week to discuss whether theirs was a service that could help Harry. If it was, the best she could offer for the moment was to add him to a waitlist for when a place opened up once lockdown lifted.

ABA stands for applied behaviour analysis and is a form of behaviour therapy developed in the 1960s with the aim of teaching language to autistic children and reducing severe behaviours. It is widely considered by experts to be the most effective therapy for autism, particularly among pre-school children. It consists of intensive one-on-one therapy with a recommended minimum of twenty hours a week, going up to forty hours a week. An individualised program is designed for each child by a program supervisor, ideally a BCBA or someone supervised by a BCBA. The program is then delivered by behaviour therapists, known as BTs, who are trained by the program supervisor on the specific steps necessary to teach new skills, or teach desirable behaviours to replace the undesirable ones.

Data collection for each behaviour is a key part of ABA therapy, and this set it apart from all the other therapies we had done with Harry. Up until we started ABA, the other therapies we tried followed a similar format. A professional met with Harry and made observations, formed a view or made a *diagnosis* of sorts—anxiety or defiance perhaps— and then applied a treatment based on a theory to address it. Success depended upon the correct diagnosis, which in turn depended upon the child displaying the *classic* signs of an overarching condition, and the correct selection of treatment. Then there was a commitment made to the treatment approach and when it didn't work, we, the parents, gave up rather than give the professional an opportunity to try their second-line treatment. Or perhaps the lack of success was attributed to a lack of consistency by the parents. Either way, each professional usually got just one shot at getting it right before the family moved on.

ABA, I was to discover, involves the detailed collection of data prior to the development of a program that is broken down to a very granular level. A program supervisor observes the child and prompts for an extensive range of different skills and behaviours, observing the environment immediately before, during and after the behaviour. Each behaviour is addressed individually. There is no attempt to look at a cluster of behaviours and label them as a condition. Instead, each behaviour is identified as stemming from one of four possible *functions* of behaviour—to escape, to get attention, to get a tangible reward or to seek sensory input. A program is then developed to address that single behaviour, bearing in mind the function of that behaviour. The program is taught to the child by the behaviour therapists who record data on the success or failure of each teaching attempt. Over time, the data is tracked and either it is successful and continued until the skill is mastered, or fine-tuned until a successful method is found. There are opportunities to review and fine-tune the strategy for each behaviour in each session. It is possible to continually tweak components of the program for mistakes without throwing out the entire program. If they get it wrong during the assessment and it turns out a child is hitting themselves in the head for attention rather than for sensory input, then the program for that behaviour is rewritten without affecting the rest.

When my research first led me to this understanding, I formed no opinion about whether this therapy would be effective with Harry. I mean, there were just so many behaviours to address. How would they even embark upon such a mission? My baseline understanding of behaviour modification was zero, but I knew this was going to be different to everything else we had tried, and few of those other things had worked. By that point, we had seen two speech therapists, two occupational therapists, two dieticians, three psychologists and three paediatricians. It was becoming increasingly difficult to find the motivation to explain Harry's unbending intent to control and avoid again and again, knowing that nobody really believed the full extent of our story.

In my mind, what all these people involved with him needed was an immersive marathon experience into the mind-bending world of Harry. In contrast to any other therapy we had experienced, ABA would be data-backed by the individual child who was being treated. He would have his own team who would spend regular and prolonged sessions with him. They would have no choice but to gain an intimate insight into our living reality with Harry. We would be believed.

Overwhelmingly, the literature indicated that ABA was highly successful, particularly when commenced intensively at a pre-school age. So why then, in my research, was I encountering so much controversy and negative commentary about it? It became clear that these voices belonged to autistic adults who had experienced ABA therapy as children. As a parent, it was impossible not to read their accounts and arguments against ABA without granting the most solemn regard to their lived experience.

My mind sorted their objections into three main reasons. The first was deeply rooted in the history of ABA, in its origins. When ABA was initially developed in the 1960s and 1970s, autism was poorly understood or tolerated. The term neurodiversity would not be coined for another twenty years. The grandfathers of ABA therapy had well-intentioned, but now outdated, objectives to make autistic children look normal and indistinguishable from their peers. This included eradicating behaviours which were harmless but looked autistic, such as flapping hands and other repetitive movements called stimming that many autistic people use for self-soothing and regulating. These days, ABA programs are designed around teaching functional skills needed for everyday living, such as eating, hygiene and toileting. Just like every other therapeutic practice ever created, ABA has been, as it should have been, refined since its inception.

A second objection was to the use of punishment. ABA uses positive reinforcement to reward desirable behaviour. Reinforcement is a consequence that strengthens a behaviour and increases the likelihood of the behaviour occurring, for example, through verbal praise, or a reward such as a toy. Early ABA also used punishment as negative reinforcement, including physical punishment, to discourage undesirable behaviour. Modern ABA no longer uses punishment. Had I been an autistic adult who endured punishment in ABA therapy as a child, I too would hold a grudge against ABA for life and close my mind off to the progress and refinements made to the practice over time. But I was not. I was an impartial observer and understood that ABA back then had utilised means that were acceptable for that time. If I could get comfortable that ABA now utilised means that were acceptable for this time, I was not willing to let bad history detract from otherwise good science.

The third main objection I came across was in relation to the intensity of the time commitment required for successful delivery of ABA, with a recommended minimum of twenty hours per week. Research demonstrated that fifty per cent of autistic children who received early ABA therapy for forty hours per week ultimately achieved normal intellectual and educational outcomes, compared to only two per cent of children who received ten hours of ABA therapy per week. Other research also indicated that children who received ABA therapy exclusively had significantly greater treatment gains than those receiving ABA combined with other therapies such as occupational therapy or special education. There no longer even existed such a thing as doing a little bit of ABA.

The size of the commitment made Paul and I baulk on multiple levels. First, we baulked at the idea of putting Harry through twenty hours per week of something that still, despite our thorough research, seemed to have all the dignity associated with reward-based dog training. Harry napped for at least forty-five minutes in the middle of the day, sometimes longer, and was often not fully *compos mentis* until some forty-five minutes after that. All that energy he expended on resisting the demands of everyday living needed to be replenished somehow. He took inordinate amounts of time to eat tiny portions of food. We allowed for approximately three hours per day for the purposes of him picking away at pitiful amounts of food. He also liked to play, and when the world opened for business again, we didn't want to deny him the opportunity to do that. He was only two years old, and play was the whole point of toddlerhood. Where would we find a spare twenty hours to fit in therapy?

Next, we baulked at the commitment for ourselves. Someone would need to stop working to facilitate all this therapy, and not just for a few months or even a year, but for the entirety of Harry's pre-school years and possibly beyond. ABA was intended to be one-on-one therapy without requiring input from a parent, so in theory, a child could be left in the care of a BT for two or three hours at a time while parents continued to work—still a logistical nightmare, but possibly viable for some. The reality for us was that Harry's anxiety was so severe that one of us would need to actively participate in the therapy with him because he would need to be physically attached to us to have any chance of cooperating. He would likely be sitting on our lap or holding our hand, at least for the foreseeable future. No grandparent or nanny was going to be an acceptable alternative. We awkwardly sidestepped this conversation about whose career was going to have to give and deferred it until our intake meeting with Tineke.

Finally, I baulked at the financial commitment. As a guide, in 2020 an ABA program of twenty hours a week came in at over 100,000 dollars a year. As an insurance scheme, funding under the NDIS was not means tested. Instead, it was based on what was considered reasonable and necessary to meet disability support needs. Harry's funding varied significantly over the years, but in the early years ranged from covering about fifty to seventy per cent of his actual ABA fees. It was an amount of funding that would have been sufficient had we been doing weekly therapies such as psychology or occupational therapy, but not ABA.

ABA was a cost and a time commitment that was likely prohibitive for many families. Ultimately, whatever form of therapy we chose for Harry, the burden remained a heavy one. We had done disparate appointments at various allied health providers before, and the logistical planning and travel required to make it work had presented plenty of its own challenges that may have eventually required me to give up my job, anyway. There was no easy solution, but at least we were fortunate that on Paul's income alone we could still afford the tens of thousands of dollars above the NDIS funding required for ABA.

So far, I had managed to reconcile two out of three of the stumbling blocks, had somewhat accepted the third, and was gravitating towards ABA for Harry until I unexpectedly came across a fourth impediment which threatened to derail all my meticulous reasoning. ABA was a banned topic on the online PDA forums I was a part of—it was considered that much of a trigger and an offence to the autistic adults who were part of the groups. Occasionally, new members to the forums unfamiliar with the rule asked whether anyone had tried ABA for their child. This would spark a thread of lengthy and sometimes aggressive commentary, ultimately resulting in a moderator's reprimand and a reminder that ABA was not to be discussed.

One particular statement that came up with concerning regularity was that ABA, like most strategies used for other autistic children, simply did not work with PDA and would likely make it worse. My heart sank. Unlike all the other criticisms about ABA where the passage of time had revised the objectionable components, and where I as a parent would have ultimate control over what was taught to my child, there was no way to get around the fact that demands were at the very heart of ABA.

ABA was the antithesis of a low-demand environment. Harry would be requested to perform all sorts of tasks in order to learn new skills. Presumably, the requests would be delivered in a fun and engaging way, but even if they brought puppies in for him to play with, the mere request for him to pat the puppy would immediately result in resistance. He simply did not have the ability to do anything that was asked or expected of him. Furthermore, assuming he accidentally patted a puppy, or was tricked into patting one, they would then presumably praise him for it. We had entire meltdowns occur simply due to the absent-minded giving of praise. If you've ever wanted to become exquisitely discombobulated, then I invite you to read some literature on PDA and praise. It seems that praise itself is capable of being perceived as a demand to repeat or improve on a previous performance—it increases the expectation!

We finally had our intake meeting with Tineke and the co-owner and business director of the clinic, Sarah. We had arranged for the call to take place during Harry's nap time, the only time Paul and I could be on a video call together without the certainty of Harry coming in to hang it up. Tineke was warm and reassuring. Sarah reminded me of myself. She was pointed and efficient, and as she would soon reveal, also the mother of a child who had done ABA years earlier. I was immediately interested in what this woman had to say. She must have been in a situation not too dissimilar to mine. What kind of black magic had she used to get from that point to this one, where she had found the capacity to run a business?

'I know how stressful it is to feel like you are walking on eggshells around your child the entire time, trying to make sure nothing you do sets them off,' Sarah said sympathetically. 'Many of the families that find us do so soon after getting their diagnosis. They are lost and just want to feel like they are doing something that might help. It will feel better once you start seeing the therapy at work.'

It occurred to me in that moment that I was much like a naive young girl nursing a broken heart, who had stumbled into a tarot reader that was saying all the things she wanted to hear, which were also all the right things to make her believe. Oh, I so wanted to believe.

ABA has a predatory approach to parents, the critics had said. This warning echoed in my mind. Sarah's words unexpectedly stirred my emotions. It was the first time anyone had shown such piercing and genuine insight into our struggles. They were words from a stranger with whom I shared a common bond. Someone out there understood.

I was testing for it, but our intake interview didn't feel predatory. Tineke and Sarah weren't trying to sell ABA to us. Much of the interview was spent with them sizing us up to see if we were suitable candidates to be accepted into their program. There were a lot of prerequisites for new intakes. They only accepted pre-school children as new learners, although they continued to work with those children into their school years. They wanted to be sure that Harry actually held a formal diagnosis, and that we understood the kind of minimum commitment required to make the program succeed.

'When you are teaching desirable behaviours and rewarding those behaviours with positive reinforcement, do you find that this approach works for kids that just want control?' Paul's voice cut through my thoughts. 'I'm not sure if you've heard of pathological demand avoidance, but we really feel that Harry fits the profile. He's hard-wired to fight every demand and more than any other reward, control is the highest prize.'

I saw Tineke's face switch to thinking as her eyes looked up and away from the screen.

'Yes, we do see that in some of the children we work with.' Her voice lacked a little confidence, but her words didn't falter. 'When the child just wants control, we can usually still find something to work with. We give choices—the choice between activities or a choice between rewards—to give back a sense of control. If Harry has special interest areas, that can really help us to set up motivating choices.'

All we needed at that point was hope, and Tineke held out just enough of it.

Now it was my turn to fire off the question that had been brewing in my mind for the past week.

'What do other families you work with do to manage ABA and job commitments? Does it usually involve a parent giving up their job to coordinate everything?'

This time there was a longer pause before Tineke replied.

'There's a bit of a combination. Sometimes grandparents can help out. Right now, with lockdown, many parents are finding they can work online while their child is in session ... but it sounds like you are struggling to work with Harry in the house. But yes ... we have a lot of learners who suffer from anxiety, especially at the start of their ABA journey. It does sound like with Harry it would be better if one of you was with him.'

I had my answer. Happy Oak required a minimum commitment of fifteen hours per week which seemed far more achievable than the standard twenty to forty hours. But even so, it appeared impossible to fit both our jobs around the hours that remained.

We had completed the interview. We got the impression they were willing to take Harry on, but were unable to offer an immediate place. We would need to join a waiting list that was going to stay stagnant until the lockdown lifted. Paul and I discussed ABA intermittently for the remainder of that second lockdown, debated whether it would be able to get past Harry's PDA. It was only a means to pass the time and both of us knew we didn't need to weigh up the merits any further. Even if ABA didn't yield any results, Tineke and Sarah did not appear to be two people capable of doing any harm. On the contrary, they had demonstrated a greater insight and understanding of our situation than any of our other therapists. We had tried all the other options available and made little progress. We had to at least give ABA a try. It was one thing to talk about neurodiversity and hope that one day the world would warmly accept Harry with all his quirks, but for Paul and me, his differences had become the least of our problems. He was simply not a functional human being for his age, and rapidly becoming less so as time wore on.

During the months of lockdown, Paul and I were two of millions of Victorians binging on streaming services. We shared a love for nature documentaries and found ourselves watching a lot of them. Against the backdrop of David Attenborough's voice, I wondered what would have become of Harry had he been a gazelle born into the herd on the screen. He wouldn't have fed when the other gazelles fed, or run in the same direction as the rest of the herd to flee from prey. He wouldn't have taken cues to shelter or rest. He would have died.

Instead, he was lucky to have been born to us, in the human world. It was 2020 and disability and autism advocacy groups were decades into their campaign to build awareness and acceptance. His future was hopeful, but we could not possibly be so idle as to just sit and wait for the world to finish its woke revolution. In case progress in his lifetime was not enough to be meaningful and sufficient, we had to forge ahead. We had to find a way to teach him the skills he needed to function within the world as it was.

THE RESIGNATION

It was October 2020 and Melbourne was still under Stage Four restrictions, but by now new cases had dipped down to single digits and a few of the most stringent requirements had been eased. The two-hour exercise limit had been removed, allowing for unlimited time outdoors. Groups of ten people across two households were permitted to meet outside. Playgrounds reopened. Our favourite neighbours across the street hosted a driveway party. We were permitted to travel up to a twenty-five-kilometre radius which meant our world over the past three months suddenly got twenty-five times bigger. The weather had improved, and we took this opportunity to take the kids to parks and playgrounds further afield.

I had old friends from university living abroad who had been visiting their families in Melbourne in July when the borders had closed. They had effectively become stuck here with their two kids when they had not mobilised fast enough before international flights were grounded. Now that schools were returning to onsite teaching, their kids were enrolled at a primary school close to the grandparents' house where they were all holed up. They suggested meeting after school at a playground close by. I was on Harry duty that afternoon and we needed an activity to stave off the cabin fever. I hadn't seen my friends the entire time they had been trapped here, and I knew they would be off at a moment's notice when travel resumed. I wrestled with whether to go. It had been so long since Harry had interacted with a child other than Tessa, and even that frequently broke out into violence. But I have a propensity for picking spontaneous moments to march headlong into certain defeat while thinking I am, in fact, tackling my fears head on, only for the truth to be revealed at the very last moment. So, I went.

I parked the car across the street, glanced over to the enclosed playground teeming with children, and immediately realised I had made a bad decision. By then, Yumi had spotted me and waved enthusiastically, so I had no choice but to bravely take Harry by the hand and forge ahead. I envied how seamlessly her young sons had taken to a new school in a new country, even the ease with which they interacted with all these unfamiliar kids running around. Harry clung to me like glue. I was unable to let go of his hand. He didn't like me speaking to Yumi and did not want to be introduced to her or her sons. He pulled me away and dragged me over to the slide. Since playgrounds reopened, he had followed Tessa down a slide once and was now obsessed with them. Up and down we went, playing exclusively on the slide for close to an hour. I was the only adult actually on the play equipment. All the other parents had congregated to exchange traumatic stories about homeschooling.

Harry had brought his favourite toy, Bun-Bun, with him, as well as his new knickknack for the day, a small rubber Iggle Piggle from the popular kids' television show, *In the Night Garden*. He created a repetitive game of taking Iggle Piggle with him down the slide, burying it in tan bark at the bottom, digging it out and taking it back down. Leo, the eldest of Yumi's sons, approached.

'Can I have a go at hiding Iggle Piggle?' he asked.

I held my breath. Here was a kid a few years older than Harry who had taken it upon himself to draw Harry into play. I found myself wishing he hadn't made that nice gesture because there was no way Harry was going to let him touch Iggle Piggle. Playgrounds were a hotbed for meltdowns each time a lockdown lifted. Children were bursting with unbridled enthusiasm, but even the most socially gifted of them had become unpractised in playground politics. Before I knew it, Leo reached down and touched Iggle Piggle! Harry shrieked like an injured animal and grabbed it back. His speech was continuing to improve and was frequently excellent, but in moments of anxiety or excitement he lost the ability to speak.

I knew I had about five seconds to avoid a full meltdown in front of Yumi and the other unsuspecting families. Harry was about to interrupt everybody's joviality, but mainly, I was worried that Leo was going to think he had done something wrong. Leo had noticed the isolated child and come over to include him. I wanted this kid to be applauded, not to feel guilty. My mind searched frantically for a solution, then I remembered in my pocket I was carrying Makka Pakka, also a character from *In the Night Garden*. I had been saving it to use as bait if I had trouble getting Harry into the car at the end of the afternoon. I threw it out onto the tanbark.

'How about Leo hides Iggle Piggle and you and Makka Pakka go find him?'

Harry weighed up the proposal for a moment, then the distress on his face was replaced by a wide, toothy grin and dimples. The meltdown was averted. Makka Pakka was a few hours newer than Iggle Piggle so Harry wanted him more. The PDAer's love of novelty salvaged the day. An hour later, when it was time to go home, I would pay the price for the premature discharge of Makka Pakka, eventually having to call Paul to delay dinner by half an hour due to my inability to get Harry back into the car.

It was late October and the end of lockdown number two felt near. Stay at home orders were finally lifted on 28 October, 111 days after they started, although extensive social distancing requirements and a restriction on travel between metropolitan Melbourne and regional Victoria remained. I got a phone call from Sarah at Happy Oak the day this was announced. I was one of about thirty people who had gathered at an outdoor bouldering wall and was taking a break between routes. Climbing on artificial surfaces was a Petrie dish for germs. I brought hand sanitiser and wore a facemask, but it was all for show to look like a responsible adult. I couldn't have cared less about catching COVID-19. After 111 days of life in captivity, like most people, I had far more pressing mental health needs than staying COVID safe. Indoor climbing gyms had still not reopened but outdoor bouldering walls were back, and they were a hive of activity as anxious climbers immediately flocked to them to rebuild their precious finger strength. I ran to a quiet spot a distance away so I could hear Sarah over the hubbub of the young bouldering crowd.

'We have a place to offer you starting late November. There are really limited places at the centre because of social distancing so we can only run in-home sessions for new clients. If it works for you, we can send one of our program supervisors to conduct the initial assessment with Harry in the second week of November.'

'Yes, we'll take it,' I said immediately. I grabbed my climbing shoes and my chalk bag and hastily left to go back home and tell Paul the good news.

Paul's relief was palpable. He could continue his leave arrangements to get us through to the end of the year, but he would be under pressure to return to public work by January. There would be an enormous backlog of medical procedures by then. Victorians had delayed their surgeries and non-urgent medical procedures for most of the year now. There had already been extensive waits in the public hospital system prior to the pandemic and many of those people had been silently growing cancers and delaying treatment for diseases through no fault of their own. Even with lockdown lifting, it would be a slow return to full capacity. Paul's job was socially more important than mine. It also brought in significantly more income and was far easier to ring-fence as a time commitment than mine as a lawyer. The NDIS funding would partially cover the cost of ABA, but for the next few years we would need to be prepared to fund tens of thousands of dollars on top of that ourselves. We had to prepare ourselves to go backwards financially for an unknown period of time. From both a social and financial standpoint, there was no need to have a discussion over who would quit their job. I knew it and had accepted it, but for some reason I fought the timing of it anyway.

It felt like a really important last battle to save my career. I didn't want to quit in January. I wanted to serve out a full twelve months and finish at the end of March. I wasn't contracted to do twelve months and could resign at any time with four weeks of notice, but I felt enormous professional guilt. I had never been a disappointment before and now I feared that was exactly what I was going to be. I had wasted my boss's time. I had gone through a triple interview process and wowed them all into believing that I was competent enough to juggle a challenging job with my two small children, convinced them that I had the expertise and intellect to do a five-day-a-week job in four. They had paid a recruitment fee to hire me and now I was leaving ten months later, and they would need to do it all again. Had I even added any value to the team in that time? Was I worth the trouble? I just wanted to know I was worth the trouble.

My sterling legal career up until that point hid a thinly veiled lack of confidence that pervaded every part of my life. I knew I wasn't actually as good as I had everyone believing. I had fluked and charmed my way through my early career with a handy combination of being just smart enough, just fun enough and just good looking enough to convince everyone that I was a fantastic deal when sold as an entire package. Now, at the point where things got hard, I had fallen apart. Was it even Harry, or was I just using him as an excuse? It would be another lengthy break before I could work again. In the best-case scenario, I was going to end up with a CV that had essentially four years out of the work force with a ten-month stint in between.

Paul wasn't having any of it. He pointed out that I was having a terrible time, festering in a special kind of hell working from home with a kid on the spectrum melting down in the background of every Zoom meeting. I had to quit in January, to literally spend my days holding Harry's hand, Paul insisted. It had to happen exactly when he went back to work. There was no one else who could fulfil this duty, even for two months.

Big Tessa's role was to take little Tessa out of the house on excursions and activities and leave the house free of distractions for Harry and the BTs, coming back only during nap times. Someone had to stay with Harry for therapy. My parents could not do it. Harry had not taken a liking to my dad who could never understand what he was saying, and my mum's conviction that she already understood ABA therapy and could run it herself was just going to result in irritating interference from her throughout the session. Paul's parents had been out of the picture for most of the year. The novelty of seeing them on the iPad for a nappy change had long worn off. They would be strangers to him once again with rapport building to take an unknown length of time.

I was squeezed out of a choice and reluctantly I resigned, giving notice until January 2021. I told Mike about Harry's diagnosis and our acceptance into an ABA program—he had seen and heard enough of Harry's behaviour on our conference calls that he didn't seem surprised. I don't know how he felt about my resignation. Given the circumstances, I never really got to know him, but he said all the right things and didn't let me feel like a great disappointment.

THE GREAT OBSERVATION

It was November 2020 and Australia was virtually free of community transmission of COVID-19. Victoria recorded consecutive days of zero new cases. I was still working from home, trying to give everything I had in my dying days of employment to hopefully make my team think I had been worth it. Shops and services reopened, and Big Tessa and Paul were able to take the kids out for lengthier periods, giving me some of my most pleasant days in the job. It was spring, and the four of them went to the zoo, Harry walking around in his socks or being carried by Paul. It was the first proper excursion of the year, the kind where you have the great privilege of paying some money to experience something that you cannot otherwise just do in the backyard. Everyone's mood had improved with the lifting of lockdown. In a week, Sophie, the program supervisor, was coming to conduct Harry's assessment.

One morning, Big Tessa was preparing to take little Tessa out to a play centre when Harry suddenly walked up and calmly announced, 'I want to go with Big Tessa today.'

Taken aback, Paul and I looked at each other, then at Big Tessa who smiled and shrugged obligingly.

'I'm happy to go with whoever wants to go with me,' she said with an ease that helpfully disguised the significance of the moment. She knew Harry hadn't left the house with anyone other than Paul or me for over four months. Most likely she had also gathered that he had never before used words to make such a request. This unexpected and pivotal event had materialised with little warning and caught the three adults off guard. The expectation hung heavily in the air as Harry waited patiently for someone to respond to him.

Paul knelt down to Harry's eye level.

'If you go with Big Tessa, you are going on your own, okay? I will take little Tessa to do something else. Big Tessa is not going to carry you. Do you understand?'

Harry nodded.

We looked at Big Tessa. She must have been nervous, but she remained a vision of calm. It was one thing to entertain Harry from the relative safety of home, but taking a seventeen-kilogram autistic toddler out for the first time was an entirely different matter. We briefed her. He needs a bottle of milk every two hours. If he has a meltdown, offer him a bottle straight away. Don't forget Bun-Bun. Offer him food while you're in the car. Here is the nappy bag. Give him your phone and let him choose something on YouTube if you need to do a nappy change, but cross your fingers you won't have to. Here is a secret little bag of surprises if you need to bribe him or distract him. Ring me if you need help!

I nervously watched as Harry climbed into the back of the car and uncharacteristically waited to be clipped into his seat. Then Big Tessa reversed the car out of the driveway and drove off. Paul had taken our second car to go to the swimming pool with little Tessa, but I had quietly whispered to Big Tessa to call me if things got out of hand, and I would jump into a cab to meet them.

Harry had decided he wanted to go with Big Tessa that day. It had been on his terms, and I shouldn't have been surprised that he followed through with it. He had watched little Tessa go with Big Tessa time and again and heard what they got up to while they were out. He had processed it and thought about it and finally, when the time was perfect, he decided he wanted to do it too. I had my phone next to me all morning, but I never got a call. They came back and had had a fantastic time. They had even gone shopping. He proudly held up a small green Ooshie. I took a closer look. It was the Incredible Hulk.

Harry had never seen the Incredible Hulk before, but this angry green man with oversized muscles, ripped purple pants and *bare* feet, he deliberately pointed out to me, captivated him.

Next time I took him with me on a supermarket trip he rode in a trolley.

'Hulk! Hulk!' he yelled excitedly, pointing his finger at some shelves.

I had just pushed the trolley past a shelf stocked with school lunchboxes and drink cups with straws. Among them were some featuring the Incredible Hulk.

'Oh yeah, it's Hulk,' I said dismissively as I tried to keep walking past.

Harry started to spiral into the early stages of a meltdown. He wanted to look at them. He wanted one of them. I walked backwards, grabbed a Hulk drink cup and threw it in the shopping trolley. Back at home, I inspected the drink cup. The straw was thick, the kind you would use for a smoothie. I had tried smoothies before. When Harry had stopped eating all his fruit, I had tried blending some into a smoothie. He hadn't completely rejected it, but he would have a few small sips and not like it quite enough to be bothered persisting. I gave it another try and made a strawberry and banana smoothie and put it into the cup. It worked! Harry's face lit up with delight as he saw the Hulk cup and he drank a third of it without question and possibly without much cognition. He was preoccupied with whether the level of the smoothie had gone down to the Hulk's gigantic biceps or to the first rip in his purple pants. This had been his first intake of fruit in close to two months. After the first few times, the smoothies in the Hulk cup ceased to work as effectively. The novelty wore off. I bought a second Hulk cup and began to challenge him to a smoothie race. Every few times I brought out the Hulk cup, I needed to find a way to use it differently from the time before if I wanted to keep Harry engaged.

Since discovering PDA, I had become attuned to the power of novelty and harnessed it to some extent to help Harry through daily transitions. Up until this point, Harry's interests had been in objects rather than in characters, and the novelty of new objects wore off pretty fast. For example, he liked trains, but this hadn't stretched to a fondness for Thomas the Tank Engine. Therefore, playing trains with Harry had been a repetitive and stunted process, rather than a creative one, extremely boring for everyone other than Harry. His play was limited to repeating the same movements with the train until the novelty wore off, after which he barely looked at the train again. But with the Incredible Hulk, the opportunist within me sprung to life.

I had always had a knack for observation. It was possibly my most innate skill. I was particularly good at picking out patterns of behaviour in people and subtle early shifts in those behaviours. I grew up going to a single sex school but at university, armed with an entirely new friendship group and freely mingling with the opposite sex for the first time, I realised how adept I was at picking up who was crushing on who long before anyone else had a clue. I could also pick out who was going to be friend-zoned or dumped, and who was just being used for their Constitutional Law notes, with uncanny accuracy. I noted the accidental brush past the shoulder and every centimetre someone stood too close. This was my superpower and now I applied it to my son.

Harry was highly habit forming. If I observed something occur two days in a row, it was bound to become a habit by the third day. He often built on a habit and made it more elaborate, but habits were hard to simplify. I could only assume that something in his mind was searching for and seeking comfort in routines and rituals. His poop ritual was the first behaviour pattern that I really used back at him to successfully prompt him to begin the process each night.

Now I experimented and found that if he was drinking a bottle of milk, I was able to slide in a Hulk smoothie as soon as he finished because his lips were still wanting to suck away. By the time he realised what I had done, he was generally able to continue because he liked the cup enough. I surreptitiously reduced the volume of milk so he would take in more of the smoothie. I let him watch clips of The Incredible Hulk to facilitate the smoothie transition. That became our new ritual, to have some milk followed by a smoothie while watching the Incredible Hulk on YouTube—not an age-appropriate choice for a three-year-old, but I willingly used what was available to me as a way to sneak in some nutrition. I added to the ritual by offering some snacks afterwards, and because he wanted to keep watching the iPad, he ate them since he had associated the iPad with eating or drinking. Soon, the process no longer needed to be carried out with such great stealth. I was able to step away to do some chores and switch over from one step in the ritual to another, even with a small break in between, because Harry had come to adopt it as his new eating ritual.

With ABA due to commence at the end of the month, I realised that to give it a chance of success I would need a clear list of Harry's special interests so the therapists could come up with a range of rewards as reinforcement for learning new skills. If each reward could only be used once or twice before the novelty wore off, that was going to become expensive. One strategy to manage that was to take a reward out of circulation and bring it back at a later time, with a fresh burst of novelty factor attached. What would be better was if a special interest, such as a character, could be re-purposed into different rewards. I began to plant the seed.

At the supermarket, I saw shampoo and bubble bath bundled together in Hulk and Spiderman bottles. That was the first moment it dawned on me that they were even friends. I had never read a Marvel comic or seen an Avengers movie. At bath time that night, I held up the Hulk shampoo and told Harry he was due for a hair wash since it had been over ten days since the last one. To my surprise he roared, 'Okay! You are Spiderman, wash my hair' and scrunched up his face into the Hulk's scowl. He accepted the hair wash with me as Spiderman squirting the shampoo like webs into his hair, growling, 'Hulk smash!' the entire time.

A dose of reality struck when I needed to rinse his hair, the most objectionable part of the entire process. He didn't quite break character, but as he obsessively demanded I dry his hair with a towel, a whiney, desperate whimper crept into the Hulk's guttural growls.

'Still wet! Some here! Eh ... Here! Aaah ...'

He continued pointing to arbitrary spots on his head. His face was scrunched, nostrils flared. Finally, he was satisfied that his hair was dry and sat back in the tub to play with the bath paint. He resumed a normal voice.

'I'm Bruce Banner,' he announced, referring to Stan Lee's fictional character of a scientist who, as a result of exposure to gamma radiation, transforms into the Incredible Hulk whenever he gets angry.

'Gamma rays,' he said, pointing to the green bath paint he had streaked across the tub.

My earliest understanding of autism was that all children on the spectrum were very literal and therefore could not be creative. Harry's inflexibility with routines certainly compounded my belief about this, since he did not accommodate any kind of fluidity or deviations in life. However, with the PDA profile of autism, one of the frequently cited quirks is that many children are, in fact, comfortable in role play. They may use it creatively as an excuse to avoid the demands of everyday life, or sometimes to help them meet the demands of everyday life. For example, a child may refuse to walk somewhere because they are a mermaid. Mermaids don't have legs and cannot walk. Conversely, I had observed the odd occasion where Harry had used his Bun-Bun as an instrument to perform a task he had originally refused, such as when requested to put something in the bin. In these situations he was always at pains to point out to me that it was Bun-Bun who had done it.

With the arrival of the Hulk, I saw an opportunity. With some adult manipulation, it was possible to use role play to meet some of the demands of reality through the use of an alter ego so that it wasn't really Harry complying with the demand. We contributed to building a rich fantasy world by addressing him as the Hulk. Sometimes we assumed the role of Spiderman or Captain America and asked for the Hulk's preferences on how to meet a certain demand, speaking as Avenger to Avenger. Within days, Harry spent most of his waking hours in character, growling away his answers.

The Hulk's usefulness did have limits. We could not, for example, suggest that the Hulk eat a burger or even a piece of bread, but we could challenge the Hulk to at least finish a chicken tender in which case Harry would savagely bite into a mouthful of chicken tender, complete with sound effects. The Hulk remained very fond of his Bun-Bun and when Sophie, the ABA program supervisor, came in to conduct his assessment, we introduced Harry to her as the Hulk and he in turn held up Bun-Bun and growled menacingly, 'And this is Bun-Bun.' He was dead serious. He didn't growl and then turn around to us and shyly giggle about it. He stayed in character all day, every day, for months. If we slipped and called him Harry, he would growl back, 'Who's Harry?'

For the first time ever, I had some influence over Harry and could even have a little two-way fun with him. So far, as parent and child, it had been a purely one-way dynamic. He demanded. I gave. In character as two Avengers, there was some give and take, something I had never experienced with Harry before. We were suddenly speaking the same language. He was a hilariously adorable little Hulk, passionate and committed. I was turning thirty-nine and suddenly I was immersed up to my eyeballs with *The Avengers*. I bought a guide to understanding the Avengers. I found myself the owner of the *Marvel Hero Collection*, an illustrated box set of stories featuring Hulk and his best friends. I read them to Harry, sometimes excruciatingly reading his favourite page over and over again at his request. I forced myself to read the other pages in my spare time. I made myself a subject matter expert on the Avengers, and Harry looked up to me for it. I answered his questions about where Iron Man's superpowers came from and whether Thor's brother was good or bad. I fed him titbits of information in exchange for compliance with a nappy change or getting into the car without a fight.

We established something that resembled a working relationship and at some point, he must have decided it was pretty cool that Mama seemed to know so much about the Avengers. Best of all was the amount of merchandise available. I gathered it all. I observed that Harry gravitated towards the bad guys. He was intrigued by the supervillains, or destructive heroes like the Hulk. When we first introduced him to *Toy Story*, his favourite character was not Woody or Buzz Lightyear like every other child. It was the Evil Emperor Zurg, the obscure villain, a minor character, that Buzz was fighting an intergalactic battle against. Harry was just different to other children at a base level. He either recognised our reluctance to allow him ready access to these villainous characters, or perhaps understood that they were hard to find, both of which made him want them even more. They were a higher currency, they were a novelty, and as inappropriate as it was for a child who was not quite three, he was soon the owner of Venom and Thanos action figures.

Sophie came to conduct his assessment using a tool known as the Verbal Behaviour Milestones Assessment and Placement Program which would be used to track his progress over time. The VB-MAPP was one of two possible tools used in the assessment of young children with autism and provided a means to measure barriers to learning in those children. The results of the assessment would be used to develop the ABA learning plan and track progress against all the skills needed to achieve school-readiness, of which there was an exhaustive list. I sat no further than thirty centimetres apart from Harry the entire time of the assessment to give him the best chance of cooperating. He was asked to stack things, sort things, imitate sounds and gestures. The requests to imitate were met with blanket refusal. If Sophie had repeated those requests, it would almost certainly have provoked a meltdown. Instead, Sophie casually said, 'Oh, you don't want to do that? That's okay, you can just say "no thanks".'

Harry didn't look at her. A few seconds went by, then with his eyes still fixed on his feet, he said, 'No thanks.'

It was the first time he had used language to refuse a task and it didn't escape me how significant that was. That day, Harry refused most of the tasks requested of him, even though he likely had the ability to perform them. The graph showing the results of his assessment looked relatively poor, but one column was checked to the top. His visual perceptual skills, indicative of early maths abilities, were very strong and when Sophie had brought out puzzles for him to solve, he had started to complete them before she had made any request. The kid clearly had a sharp working mind and a desire to use it. He just didn't like being asked to use it.

During a break in the assessment, while Harry drank from his baby bottle, Paul asked Sophie, 'Have you worked with anyone like this before?'

He was fishing for some kind of validation that no one else in the world had had to face the uniqueness of this challenge we had been put up against. It was a sentiment I shared with him. We gratefully acknowledged that we did not have a child with an intellectual disability or a physical disability, both of which would have handed us an entirely different palate of challenges and burdens. We instead had something behaviourally bespoke, a young person who systematically, intelligently and creatively thwarted our every attempt to help him with the basic requirements of human existence. It felt important to have it acknowledged that we had no template of strategies to work from, that everything was based on trial and error. Sophie would not be drawn into the question.

Sophie replied with a detached professionalism, 'Each learner is different.'

Our entire experience with Happy Oak ended up based on this premise. There was never an attempt to pigeonhole Harry as a certain *type* of autistic, even if that type was PDA, as we were so ardently spruiking. There was never an attempt to find a group of strategies that could be applied wholesale to his profile. Instead, Happy Oak focused on one behaviour at a time and looked at what that one behaviour was saying.

With the assessment complete, Sophie began working with Tineke to write up Harry's program. To me, much of the program looked like general early childhood teaching with the aim being to ensure that Harry would learn all the things he needed to be school ready—developing language, identifying colours, requesting help, accepting help, getting familiar with sharing and turn taking. But the aspects of the program that most interested me were the parts designed to address specific challenging behaviours.

Paul and I had nominated three behaviours we desperately wanted help with—wearing shoes, transitions and eating. Tineke immediately deferred the eating. They had observed Harry's eating. They had conducted feeding programs for a small number of other learners before. Not many, but enough to know that severe self-restricted eating was a highly complex and sensitive set of behaviours. Starting a feeding program too early in the ABA journey could risk derailing rapport with all Harry's behaviour therapists, or BTs, and jeopardise the progress of the rest of the program.

'Can you give us a few months to get some ABA underway with him?' Tineke asked. 'Once we get to know him and he knows us a bit better, we can put something together. I know how much stress his eating is causing, but in our experience it's not a good one to get into straight away.'

Her answer made sense. It was wise. I knew it, but I didn't like it.

My life up until this point had been ruled by a sense of impatience. I was a natural timekeeper, a clock watcher. I constantly needed to get to the next milestone by a certain time, but to embark on ABA was to play the long game. Even Paul, who had spent much of the year downplaying his concerns about Harry's eating, hoping his feigned indifference would somehow rub off on me, was deflated by the news. He was exhausted by the charade but tenaciously maintained it, thinking it was the only way to hold the family together each mealtime.

By late November, the last vestiges of the second lockdown had gone. It was spring and everything seemed a little brighter. Most indoor venues could now host events of up to 150 people. Cinemas and museums were back. Life was almost normal again except that masks were still mandated everywhere outside the home. Office workers were encouraged to work remotely wherever possible. I met up with friends and discovered we no longer knew how to greet one another in person. We hovered awkwardly a metre or two apart in the space where a hug would normally have taken place and where no suitable alternative had yet developed to fill the void.

We had visitors in our home, and we visited others. Tessa wanted nothing more than to 'go to someone else's house' which became her standard response when asked what she wanted to do that day. After her first visit to a friend's home, it became a battle to walk up our street without her running up to each front door in an attempt to ring the doorbell to say hello and wave at people. She was a child naturally gifted with social skills and brimming with intuition about how to use it. She led the way. Harry followed her up the path to the door in his socks and stood a little way behind, curious but safely shielded from the initial interaction by his brave little sister.

Harry's ABA got underway just before the end of 2020. We had committed to fifteen hours per week and either Paul or I sat in close proximity to him for the entirety of his three- hour sessions. The first two weeks went exactly as we had expected. Requests to do things were met with persistent refusal from Harry, particularly for tasks such as packing up the toys after he had played with them. The BTs observed this and took their data. He would not comply with, 'Can you please pack up the Lego?' but phrased as, 'Let's see who can put the most Lego back into the box!', it was met with greater success. He protested and escaped from the room or undid whatever it was he had just done the moment he was given praise such as 'Good job!'. But he continued on with the task, sometimes dimples giving away his delight, if a BT turned to me and exclaimed, 'Oh my goodness, have you seen the awesome tunnel Harry just built over the train track?'

ABA was usually delivered one-on-one without parental input, but in Harry's case, we were very active participants since initially he refused to do anything unless we completed the task with him. We contributed observations from our home setting. We gathered and supplied reinforcers that were special interests for Harry, and we began to change tack in our daily lives to frame demands consistently with his ABA therapy. I was watchful, too, because I had resolved but not forgotten the criticisms about ABA. Was this doing any harm? Was he going to look back on this when he was a teenager and hate us for what we had signed him up for? Would he spend his adult life seeing psychologists to talk about how when he was not yet three years old, he was asked to sort out the Avengers Ooshies from the Toy Story ones and that was why in his adulthood, he refused to systematically file anything away?

I looked out for the danger, but I never saw it. Yes, he had meltdowns, protests and frequent refusals, but much less than what we normally experienced in unstructured play with him. In free play, most of our instructional language towards him manifested as 'Gentle!' or 'Not so loud!' or 'Watch out!'. It was yelled urgently after the fact, and that in itself could trigger a meltdown. In ABA, the play was structured and prompted by language that would otherwise have been reprimands had they not been delivered calmly as reminders ahead of time.

'Who can be the quietest putting the blocks away? Remember, if we pack the blocks up gently, we can have a Hulk and Thor battle.'

Meltdowns, when they occurred, usually did so as a result of reinforcers being withheld due to refusal or delay in completing a task, such as being asked to touch his nose. Sometimes it was because he didn't want to touch his nose on request, but often, with a minor request like that, it was because he could not wait to get the reinforcer and didn't want to have to undertake another task first. The BTs took data and modified the request. The task was wound back so that the request was simply to *let* Paul or me touch his nose and him letting us do that was enough to earn the reinforcer. Over time, it was built back up again until he had to touch his own nose to get the reinforcer. Eventually, he had to touch multiple requested body parts in succession to get the reinforcer. It was a significant step in practising compliance.

In the first year and a half of ABA, nearly nothing was done at the table, which had been one of my fears. I had had visions of my poor toddler sat at a table head-to-head with a therapist for hours each week. Instead, all the therapy was play based and led by Harry, conducted on the floor or running around the house in role play. It also wasn't relentlessly repetitive or oppressive in the way described by critics of the therapy. Each target was run just once per session. Harry did five sessions a week but with different BTs leading different play scenarios into the target and with different reinforcers on offer. Harry was, in fact, having the most varied and creative play experience he had ever had. Day by day, we discovered he had a colourful imagination far beyond his years. He had a talent for improvisation and, far from being literal, he was visionary, innovative and very, very funny.

The BTs learnt about his special interests. Harry still spent his days growling away as the Hulk and the BTs referred to him as such. After weeks of staying in character as the Hulk, Paul and I began to worry about him permanently damaging his vocal cords, but we were unable to bring him out of character. Sometimes he would assume other characters such as Buzz Lightyear or Woody from *Toy Story*, which he had been exposed to in ABA and grown fond of, but usually he just wanted to be the Hulk. Eventually, I suggested he could be "Happy Hulk" and talk in a happy voice. I didn't really think that would catch on, but to my surprise, he took on his normal voice while still in character as the Hulk. The catch was that we now had to refer to him as Happy Hulk, otherwise he would immediately revert to a growl. Other times, the Hulk just couldn't be happy and nothing could stop the growl. It was complicated, but I was getting the hang of Harry. I had a little leverage and had gotten a glimpse inside the chaotic and brilliant mind of my not yet three-year-old son.

Each of his four BTs came armed with their own personal bag of toys. Within two weeks of ABA starting, he was running to the door each time the bell rang to see who had arrived and which toys they had brought with them. Someone else's toys were a novelty and his interest areas continued to expand. He liked Amy the best because she had dinosaurs and volcanoes. Tori had some cool insect puzzles. We had one BT who he simply did not take a liking to. She didn't bring as many toys and knew little about the Hulk. As soon as she walked through the door, he ran away upstairs and continued to scurry around various rooms in the house, escaping her. I couldn't see that she had done anything wrong, but it occupied so much of the session just to round him up to be in the same room as her that I asked for a personnel change. Soon we had Katrina who lugged around several overnight bags filled with toys in the boot of her car and the problem was sorted.

To my surprise, after a few days of initial resistance, Harry did respond relatively well to the use of rewards as reinforcement. For it to work, the reward needed to be tangible and immediately accessible. It also needed to be highly desirable in order to motivate him to complete the task. It could not be overly desirable, though, as that would cause him to demand it in advance and thus lose track of the task at hand, or he could refuse to relinquish it at the end of the allocated time. Over time, as he got used to being rewarded, he became less suspicious of the concept of quid pro quo promised in return for the performance of a task. The use of praise as reinforcement, however, remained problematic and the BTs simply left it alone. After a year, he eventually came to tolerate more indirect and casual forms of praise such as 'Awesome, dude!' or 'You're a superstar!' but it was close to three years before he displayed any kind of motivation based on praise alone.

Harry was having such a good time during sessions that the problem became Tessa. She saw the toys. She noticed the full attention given to Harry by the visiting adult in the room and the over-the-top animated play, and she wanted to be a part of it. Big Tessa's job was keeping little Tessa occupied on excursions, but when they came home to nap in the middle of the day and saw the tail end of Harry's sessions, it was she who threw the biggest tantrums.

I felt relief. After just a month, we had no practical results yet, and one of us was tethered to Harry by his separation anxiety the entire time, but if nothing else, it was adult engagement that was being spearheaded by someone else other than Paul or me. Someone else had to rack their brains for ideas to entertain him and teach him skills he should have learnt in a childcare or playgroup setting had he been able to attend. Most significantly, I could not see how this could be harming him.

I became accustomed to the echoes of doubt which would continue to plague a small part of my mind for the rest of my life. It served as a touchstone that reminded me for the entirety of our journey with ABA to remain vigilant. As much as I felt confidence that we had chosen the right path, I remained forever on the lookout for evidence to either support or dispel it, to validate that we had done the right thing.

A month after we commenced ABA, we stopped for a three-week Christmas break. Harry was disappointed. No one was coming over for the sole purpose of playing games with him and he was reduced to playing with just his own toys and vying with Tessa for our attention. He asked where his 'teachers', as he called his BTs, had gone, and when they were coming back.

For Christmas 2020, Santa wore a facemask, meaning that in combination with his abundant beard he suffered terribly with fogged lenses. Sometimes he sat in a bubble or in a glass box. Other times, he sat at one end of his sleigh as far away as possible from the children who had come to meet him who were seated at the other end. In an especially poor set up, Santa sat atop a podium in a large red throne checking his list, while small children stood a few steps below, with the appearance of frightened peasants called before a king.

Carols by Candlelight was a long-running Melbourne tradition on Christmas Eve, a fundraising variety show held at an outdoor venue with a capacity for 10,000 people, usually filled on Christmas Eve nights by families waving candles in the night air. That year, it was held without an audience and broadcast into homes. Songs were sung by a socially distanced choir, and it was suggested that people wave candles in front of their television. Still, the quality of life had improved. Groups of thirty were allowed to gather in homes for Christmas and masks were no longer required outdoors where social distancing was possible. Paul was fly-fishing with regularity. I was back in the climbing gym trying to heed the posters cautioning over-zealous climbers to return to training carefully. It was a muted festive experience, but off the back of a year marked by confinement and depression, Victoria had just scraped in with a satisfactory finish.

BLUE SUEDE SHOES

Harry stopped wearing shoes sometime in July 2020. It started off with him fussily tearing off his shoes the moment he got into a car or home, then it turned into extended negotiations to get him to put his shoes on to go out. Soon it progressed to going out in socks when we could no longer be bothered to persist with the fight. Before we knew it, he hadn't had shoes on his feet in a month, then three months, then six months. We had chronically sore shoulders and backs from carrying Harry around. It was particularly punishing when we had to pick him up to get him somewhere safe and private while he was in the throes of a meltdown. Tessa, seeing Harry get carried around all the time, wanted to be picked up, too. Paracetamol and anti-inflammatories had become a mainstay for survival in our household, and outbursts occurred if Paul or I had taken the last of them and neglected to add them to the shopping list—an act of utmost inconsideration.

We bought all different types and colours of shoes, even hybrid shoes which were essentially socks with a rubber sole. Paul tried to custom-make some of his own using Harry's favourite socks and rubber sheets from a hardware store. Harry would touch them and play with them like toys and put them on his hands like puppets but screamed the moment we attempted to approach his feet with them. In late November, when the second lockdown eased, we had a family photography session in the Fitzroy Gardens. For reasons still unknown to me, I wanted to pretend to be a normal family and fraudulently represent that in photographic form.

Muttering short-tempered instructions to each other under our breath, Paul and I took turns carrying Harry around so he wouldn't get a prickle in his sock or step in a puddle which would have upset the entire session and sent us home. We narrowly avoided a meltdown when the photographer lured Tessa into terrain under low-hanging branches. This was difficult for us to negotiate carrying Harry and he got his socks dirty trying to follow. Printed on canvas and affixed above our staircase are moments captured from that day, Harry's dirty socks on full display. It would be April 2021, nine months after he last wore shoes, by the time he wore them again.

There was one exception to this. My electric-blue suede wedding stilettos. I had worn them one time only, under a slinky ivory wedding dress with a dainty train and bead-embellished capped sleeves. In my favourite wedding photo, which hangs in our hallway, Paul and I are running down an empty highway in the Grampians, or *Gariwerd*, the surging crest of Mt Abrupt rising directly behind us, my blue suede shoes just peeking out from under the hem which is flowing, carried along by the frivolity of a woman who had every reason to believe she was running from one phase of a charmed existence into another.

One day, I heard a clumsy, lopsided clip-clopping coming down the hall. No one in Melbourne wore heels in 2020. Who was in my house? I walked towards the sound and found Harry shuffling down the hall in my blue stilettos, grinning widely, dimples on full display. Most of his foot fell within the front half of the shoe, so he was effectively standing flat. He was holding Bun-Bun, laughing.

'Gook at me!' he cried.

Harry couldn't pronounce the "L" sound and instead substituted it for "G".

'Gook! Keep gookin'!' he cried excitedly as he spun around and did a little jig.

Soon afterwards, I heard the unmistakable happy squeal of Tessa as she emerged behind him. She was shuffling along wearing Paul's running shoes. The two of them waddled around the house side by side in their parents' shoes, cackling with delight at the sight of one another. Tessa patted her own face with both hands in excitement and Harry immediately copied her. They ran around as fast as they could in oversized footwear, clapping their hands around their faces.

That was how things went with the two of them those days. Harry was almost three and Tessa was nearing two, big enough to fend for herself. With the intense confinement of lockdown gone, they now got along tremendously. Well, half the time. Tessa had an incredible appetite for play. She had a ready laugh and was desperate for a playmate. She was used to Harry rushing up and standing too close to her, or erratically flinging out a limb in a dramatic gesture without warning. She was tough and willing to put up with whatever fallout was involved in play with Harry, but when she fought back, it was dirty. She was stocky. Pound for pound, she was much stronger than Harry, just smaller. The other half of the time they were together, there was physical evidence to vouch for it, either as damage done to one another or havoc jointly wreaked on items around the house. Scratch marks, bite marks, torn books, chipped plaster and a ripped couch. There was nothing in between—no parallel play, no sitting quietly on the couch to watch a movie.

In the weeks that ABA was on hold over the Christmas break, Harry and Tessa pulled out the shoe stunt numerous times. I reported it to Sophie as soon as therapy commenced again. She was interested. She was writing the program and that was going to be her starting point. It was to be the way Happy Oak dealt with all of Harry's challenging behaviour. They started with a task so achievable that even Harry could barely believe he was being asked to do it, let alone get rewarded for doing it.

In mid-February, the shoe program had been written and was ready to launch. I had finished up at work a month earlier and returned my laptop and phone to the office via courier. My entire career at the insurance company had been served remotely. Paul was back to his regular work schedule, and I was now a full-time carer.

Victoria entered another lockdown, its third. It was marketed as a snap lockdown, a 'short, sharp circuit-breaker,' said Premier Andrews. Scheduled for five days, it was to curb the spread of a new strain of highly infectious COVID-19 that stemmed from breaches of hotel quarantine for returned travellers. Stage Four restrictions returned, but we were established ABA clients now and that was deemed an essential service, exempted under the lockdown rules. Harry's therapy continued without disruption.

I had been asked to gather some high-value rewards which would be reserved only for the new shoe program, not as reinforcement in the rest of his ABA sessions. They would be offered on a rotating basis to Harry, taken away at the end of the session and hidden for some time, new ones brought out in their place. On the first day, Harry was asked to place one foot into one of my blue stilettos for one second. If he did that, he would get to choose between playing with a Mr Potato Head playset or a pair of enormous padded Hulk gloves for ten minutes. Harry was always given a choice of rewards. It helped give him back some sense of control in a situation where he might otherwise have felt disempowered at having to work for a reward. He completed the task with a grin and chose the Hulk gloves. The next day, Harry was asked to step both feet into the shoes for one second. The day after that, both feet had to go in for five seconds. Next, he needed to take a few steps, then walk from one room to another. The first phase was complete. All of this was accomplished without fuss and with great delight from Harry. Although my stilettoes were not useful footwear, it was a fun practice round for what was to follow.

In preparation for the next phase of the program, Sophie had asked me to purchase a pair of Crocs in Harry's size. Crocs were loose-fitting sandals with a flip-up-or-down heel strap that could be made relatively secure when the strap was flipped down. She had observed his dislike of physical prompting and assistance. He often protested and escaped in sessions when the BTs tried to physically demonstrate or assist him with tasks like washing hands or holding a pen. He did not take well to physical intervention of any kind. She thought that sneakers or dress shoes, which required the pulling open of the tongue and adult help with Velcro straps, would require too much physical involvement from someone else. But Crocs, with the heel strap flipped up, provided a generous opening for the foot to simply be stepped into it without input from anyone else. I was impressed. In her short time with Harry, she had said little but had read him with incredible subtlety.

Not only did I buy the Crocs, but I also bought an outrageous assortment of decorative gems that could be plugged into the little holes on the tops of the Crocs as decorations—we were able to customise the Crocs to his changing interests. The gems were available in a fantastic array of his favourite things: The Avengers, Toy Story characters, dinosaurs, trains, insects and cupcakes. Although he wouldn't eat real cupcakes, Harry did like all things cupcake.

Sophie had come in to supervise Taylor. As a program supervisor, Sophie attended overlap sessions with each BT once a month to monitor their teaching and to introduce new programs as existing ones were mastered. They had laid the Crocs on the floor, and Taylor began reading out the social story they always started the program with.

My name is Harry and I am three years old. I am really good at puzzles and sliding across the floor. I like the Hulk and Toy Story. I am still learning to wear shoes. Shoes are important so that I can run around in the playground and go to exciting places without hurting my feet. It would make Mama and Dada so happy if I wore my shoes.

Harry listened and looked intently at the photos of himself doing puzzles and dressed up as the Hulk. He had heard the same story for the past two weeks but sat for it attentively, anyway.

'Have a look up at the shelf, Harry,' said Taylor. 'Today you need to step one foot into one of these Crocs for one second, then you can choose from the toys up on the shelf to play with for ten minutes.'

Harry looked at the excellent choices I had put up for the session. There was a new Biro train that blew out real steam and could run along his existing train tracks. There was also an old fire truck I had found at the trash and treasure market, a little cracked but it had a ladder that swivelled around, sirens that flashed and a hose that sprayed real water. I held my breath. He danced on the spot with excitement and indecision, then eventually chose the train. He plunged his foot into the Croc and yelled, 'Give me train!'

The next time the program was run, both feet had to go into the Crocs for a second. The day after that, both feet had to go in for five seconds. Next, he needed to take a few steps. Harry stalled. He refused the task and the reward. They had moved too fast. What was being asked of him was too uncomfortable for the reward on offer to be worthwhile. Sophie saw the data and requested the BTs go back a step. His feet just needed to go in for five seconds again. They consolidated on that level for a few sessions in a row. Then he was asked to take a few steps and this time it worked. They slowed down the entire program and he spent a few days at each level. This was a desensitisation approach which would be used for Harry numerous times over the years for some of his most challenging sensory-driven behaviours.

We were now at the end of March and Sophie called for some fresh reinforcers. The crux of the program was coming up and Harry needed to walk from inside the house out into the backyard in his Crocs. I had on offer a talking Bullseye horse plush toy and Rex action figure, both from *Toy Story*. Harry chose Bullseye the horse. He stepped into his Crocs and started stiffly walking through the living room. Paul and I both looked at each other and seized the moment.

'Giddyap!' I yelled at him. Paul hopped on his pretend horse and galloped through the living room, threw open the door and ran into the backyard. Harry followed, riding Bullseye and forgetting about the Crocs on his feet. He ran into the backyard and galloped around behind Paul. Taylor followed us out, carrying her laptop and trying to point the camera at the rodeo taking place in the backyard for Sophie who was conducting the overlap session online.

Harry had developed a dislike for Sophie and started sending her out of the room when she came in for overlaps with the BTs. She had resorted to sitting on the staircase to observe, or in the adjacent room that was separated by a sliding partition, in the dark because Harry would not allow her to turn on the light. Finally, she was reduced to observing the session through a narrow gap in the sliding door. He had worked out that she was in charge and was wrestling back whatever control he could by making her jump through hoops. He knew she was instructing the BTs on what programs to run and how to run them. He may have liked the BTs, but he didn't like Sophie's authority. Realising this, she switched to supervising the BTs online. Harry galloped past on Bullseye and yelled, 'Turn it off!' to Taylor who was holding the laptop. He had worked out exactly what was going on. He indulged us sometimes when it suited him and called us out on it when it did not.

It was Saturday 10 April 2021. Autumn had made its presence known in Melbourne with a series of cool and rainy days. Paul was working that morning. Big Tessa had taken the car and driven out with little Tessa to separate the kids for a few hours. Earlier in the week, Harry had successfully worn his Crocs for a walk out onto the street, the first time out of the house in shoes for nine months. But this had been for just a few minutes in an ABA session. The skill was far from being generalised and I had not yet been given the go ahead to try it out myself. We were all still proceeding with extreme caution. Just an hour earlier, I had taken Harry out on his bike in his socks because I was too afraid to broach the issue of shoes and he hadn't offered to put them on. We were caught out in the rain and I pushed him back up the hill towards home to get changed when he started getting upset about being wet. After an hour back at the house, we needed something to do. The heavy rain had stopped but swift rivers were flowing down the gutters outside.

'Harry, I have an idea,' I said cautiously.

He liked ideas. I had his attention.

'There are little rivers running down our street right now from all the rain. Would you like to race some leaves down them?'

He probably didn't completely understand what I had in mind, but it sounded fun.

'Yes. Let's do that,' he said.

'Okay, but see how it's wet outside?'

'Yes.'

'We can't go outside unless you wear your shoes.'

'Okay, let's put on some shoes then.'

This was really happening. Nine months of coaxing, imploring, begging, despairing and carrying him around. Aching backs and shoulders. Tens of thousands of dollars of ABA therapy. An abandoned career. In that one moment, Harry was on the cusp of an act that could almost square the ledger. I was quaking on the inside, but I summoned every scrap of self-control I had to exude nonchalance. I waved a hand casually in the direction of his Crocs.

'Well, come on then. Put them on.'

He went over to them but at the last moment noticed a pair of his hybrid sock-shoes which he had rejected some six months ago. They were blue with a little orange fox on them and had lain unused in the corner of the shoe pile.

'I want these,' he said.

They were now likely too small for his feet, but I had to just work with what he was giving me.

'Okay then, let's give them a go.'

I helped him put them on. They were a little tight, but their hybrid design meant it didn't really matter for the moment. It was sufficient to keep his feet dry if he stayed on the footpath. He stood up. I opened the front door. He walked down the steps to the driveway then froze holding Bun-Bun, jaw squared and bottom teeth bared. He suddenly appreciated the gravity of the moment. My mind worked quickly. I couldn't just let him stand there and wait for uncertainty to take hold.

'Come on then, let's race the leaves!' I cried with great excitement and strode past him onto the pavement.

He was swept up in my momentum. He came forwards. He walked a few stiff-legged steps out to the footpath. I maintained my commentary and began busily looking for leaves on the ground, deliberately not paying any attention to the momentousness of the occasion. He joined me. I hastily found two leaves and we set them into the gutter, watching as they twirled and sprinted away down into the stormwater drain.

'I won! I won,' he shouted, jumping up and down on the spot. He had completely forgotten about his shoes.

It was a breakthrough moment, a breakthrough in the relationship between Harry and me, in Harry's journey with ABA, in his access to the world. After this day, shoe wearing ceased to be a problem. ABA continued with the shoe program, but it was accelerated so he was introduced to different types of shoes like runners and gumboots. The next time he went to the zoo, he ran around freely from one exhibit to the next. He delighted on riding the miniature railway, a treat that would have been denied without closed-toed shoes. He was finally able to fully participate in the playground, climb up the ladders and rope courses. With Tessa to follow around, he even began to use the play equipment in the manner intended, at least much more so than he had ever done before. Maybe he would have come around to wearing shoes under his own will one day, but without ABA intervention that looked to be a long time coming.

We remained nervous every time we had to get Harry a new pair of shoes in the next size up, or introduce him to new types of footwear. I held my breath the first time we hired climbing shoes and the first time he got fitted for ski boots. On each of those occasions, we talked about it extensively before the need arose, watched cartoons on YouTube of climbers and skiers having fun, offered a reward for compliance, and, when the day came, he tentatively but agreeably put his foot forward. He never lost the desire to tear off his shoes as soon as he entered the car or the house, but he would at least put them on when needed. I asked five-year-old Harry what the deal was with not wearing shoes for nearly a year. He remembered it. His memory was exceptional. He pointed to the back of the shoes and said, 'Too hard here on my old shoes.'

'But what about all those other shoes we got you?' I asked.

He shrugged. That was the rigidity that even Harry couldn't explain. If he got one small twist in his knickers, his default solution was to forgo knickers altogether.

TRY ANYTHING, BUT DO NO HARM

Sophie and Tineke were in no hurry to put a food program in place, instead taking their time to build rapport with Harry through more fun-filled targets. My impatience about Harry's disturbed feeding patterns had rubbed off on Paul. Throughout December, he had drawn on every iota of leverage and milked every connection he had as a doctor to find a way to get Harry into an autism-specific feeding program. A very small number of such services existed, but all had extensive waiting lists and social-distancing requirements had greatly reduced the capacity at all the clinics. Eventually, we made progress when our paediatrician made an urgent request for a placement at one of Australia's most highly regarded autism treatment centres that ran a much sought-after feeding clinic. Harry was offered a place commencing in January 2021.

At that stage, Harry was eating around ten different foods, all of which were brand specific. He ate slowly and distractedly, would refuse the food if the packaging changed and was disgusted by anything that was not of a crunchy texture. One of the treats he enjoyed was going to a McDonald's drive-through and ordering three hash browns. He would nibble his way around the crunchy rim of all of them, then hand the rest to Tessa. Sometimes the hash browns were floppy or soggy and he rejected them upon a first bite, spitting out that mouthful in disgust.

I received a call from Paul one day when he had taken Harry on a morning mission to get hash browns for breakfast. The paper sleeve in which they were served had undergone a promotional change and came with a Monopoly sticker affixed to it which could not be removed without ripping the sleeve. Harry had taken one look and cried in distress. No amount of pointing out the logo of the golden arches or explaining to him that this was the same drive-through he went to yesterday could convince him otherwise. He would not accept eating them without the sleeve either. Paul called me devastated from the car to share his distress. The desperation and loneliness in his voice seemed to emanate from a deep, dark hole in another world. It frightened me. He had tenaciously maintained that the eating situation wasn't as bad as I was making it out to be, but right then, I saw how dire he really thought it was all along. Here was a man who was afraid that his three-year-old son was determined to starve to death. The one food which Harry looked forward to eating was suddenly denied to him.

From the very first moment he set foot in the autism centre, Harry showed an intense dislike for everything about it. The small, plain treatment rooms, the mismatched playsets, the lack of extravagant playfulness by the therapists. He was highly strung the entire initial assessment and expended huge amounts of energy thwarting my attempts to speak with the two therapists who were conducting it. He attempted to control me, grabbing my face and turning it towards him, covering my mouth with his hands and protesting, 'No talking!'

I waited for the therapists to delve into their wealth of paediatric experience and distract or redirect his attention. I thought that rather than ask me about his special interests, they could ask him or engage him in boisterous and animated play, win him over with their charm. They never did. They placed a bucket of blocks in front of Harry and continued trying to ask me questions about his eating, further infuriating him. One of them invited him to play in the garden only to be puzzled by his heightened reaction to the attempt at coaxing him off my lap. I was stumped. Harry had a diagnosis of ASD Level 2. The autism centre would have seen far more severe cases than his. It began to dawn on me that his combination of autistic attributes really was that rare.

Nevertheless, we began the feeding clinic. The therapy was ABA based and conducted by a feeding-focused speech therapist. I will acknowledge straight up that she had been given a most difficult and unpleasant undertaking with Harry. We travelled to the centre once a week for fifty minutes, solely for the purposes of the food program and nothing else. Paul and I had overlooked the problem this was going to present, since the food program—one of the most unbearable tasks imaginable for Harry—was unable to be disguised or even diluted as part of a more engaging set of general ABA targets. Unlike the shoe program, it was not one of fifteen tasks he was called upon to do in a session.

Harry was seated at a small table, on my lap, next to a microwave, where the speech therapist heated a small amount of his macaroni and cheese, put it in front of him and requested he take a fork and touch it to his lips for one second. As a reward, he was given some colouring sheets with his choice of Toy Story characters and allowed five minutes to colour them in before the next task. He reluctantly did as he was asked, so long as I held his hand in my hand while he held the fork. He then coloured a picture of Cowgirl Jesse with lacklustre enthusiasm. Colouring was not a preferred task. Instead of a reward, he was being asked to perform a chore for having performed an even worse chore. Next, he was asked to touch his tongue to the macaroni and cheese. He refused the task. He wasn't interested in more colouring. A stand-off ensued. Minutes went by in uninspiring silence. The therapist went and got some different colouring sheets and a few other toys. He wasn't interested in the reward that was being offered.

'I want to go home,' he said to me. 'I want to go now.'

He wasn't distressed. He was making a statement. This wasn't fun and he wasn't going to participate. Eventually, the fifty minutes were up, and we left without him completing the task.

We went back the next week. He was given some new colouring sheets, a choice between dinosaurs and Toy Story characters. He successfully touched the forkful of food to his tongue but refused to repeat the same level again when requested to, and refused the reward. The following week, he asked where we were going as I prepared him to get into the car. When I told him, he refused. I negotiated and offered bribes. I told him we could go to his favourite play centre after, and he reluctantly agreed. We got to the feeding clinic fifteen minutes late, but that was still plenty of time for him to sit and have a stand-off with the therapist. He continued to refuse the task.

I called Sophie and confessed to her that we had started a separate feeding clinic with another centre. I asked if she could speak with the therapist there to share some insights about how they had applied ABA with Harry at Happy Oak. I could clearly see that both practices were using ABA principles, but the way one was being executed was to Harry's taste, and the other was not.

After Sophie's phone call, the feeding therapist began introducing a choice between reinforcers. Harry could have a choice of doing a puzzle or some colouring. This helped a little and he moved up one further level. However, the entire target had failed to be dressed up and marketed as something more appealing than simply putting food he found repulsive into his mouth. The task of convincing him to get into the car to go there each week became insufferable. I, too, had started to dread going to the feeding clinic and began dragging my feet until the last minute. We turned up consistently late as he looked for reasons to delay getting buckled into the car. He collected sticks and pebbles as he walked from the carpark into the building, and I acquiesced.

I was overwhelmed by a feeling of defeat each time we entered the treatment room, knowing that most of the time was going to be spent sitting in a loaded silence—the therapist and I waiting for Harry to do something, Harry fixed in a determined stand-off. What he was being asked to do was highly repetitive and boring. Success, if it was ever to be achieved, would be by an approach of wearing him down. They were trying to break him in.

My mind flicked back to all those criticisms I had read about ABA. This was reminiscent of one of my early fears about Harry being sat at a table, head-to-head with a therapist until he finally did what he was being asked to. After five months with Happy Oak, I now knew that ABA was slow but powerful. It did work. As parents, Paul and I ultimately presided over decisions about what kinds of things the tool of ABA should be applied to. That was our responsibility. In combination with their own professional judgement, the therapists acted upon our instructions. Was this doing him harm in the long run? I wasn't sure how to answer that. It certainly was devoid of any kind of childlike joy. It seemed possible that this was traumatic, not as you or I know it, but for Harry. It didn't require much imagination to see him sitting in a psychologist's office in his teens, venting about how his parents had dragged him to a feeding clinic as a three-year-old and that's why he had been caught force-feeding small animals. He was being asked to ingest food, put something in his mouth that he didn't want to, with a view to eventually eating it. Putting something in one's body is invasive. It is different to being asked to park a toy garbage truck next to a toy fire truck, or to sort out all the animals from the people in a pile of pictures. The clinic's no-frills approach to asking him to do it was only amplifying that discomfort.

Taking Harry to the feeding clinic each week didn't feel right, even though I wasn't sure what was wrong about it. Perhaps it just felt *institutional*. Doubting myself and wondering whether I was just intolerant of the boredom involved, I asked Paul to take a few mornings off work and attend the clinic with Harry.

'Oh my God!' Paul declared when he returned. 'There is no way he will be eating mac 'n' cheese in the next six months!'

'Should we pull him out?' I asked hopefully. 'It's an hour and a half of travel there and back and he just sits there for fifty minutes. Maybe we can push Happy Oak to get onto a food program now?'

Harry held a spot in one of the most coveted autism-specific feeding programs available, known for its success. The centre's webpage was filled with testimonials from families who were grateful for the feeding clinic, whose children were able to go to school and come home with empty lunchboxes. We had waited and begged for this. Sophie had told us she didn't know of any other Happy Oak families who had managed to get into the program, only many wanting a place. I couldn't believe we were on the verge of relinquishing it, but we knew this approach, successful as it may have been for other kids, was not right for Harry.

When we had first received Harry's diagnosis, our paediatrician had shared some words that lingered in my mind.

'You will be the expert in Harry more than any other expert in autism, and you will need to use that knowledge to advocate for him.'

I had worked out the answer. This was one of those moments where the usual strategies used for autism really did not work for PDA, or at least did not work for Harry. It had been worth a try but if we were to persist with it, it was possibly going to do more harm than good. We had adopted a mantra of try anything but do no harm. It was time to try something else.

I make the point of stressing that I hold no other positive or negative views about the treatment being run by the centre. Our decision was driven only by what worked for Harry and his experience of it. I understood this to be a highly esteemed treatment facility held in high regard by many of the experts we worked with. I was disappointed by the poor fit of the feeding clinic. I had placed too much hope and reliance upon it working out when I should have approached it with a mindset of possibility, nothing more. Finding the right treatment and having it delivered by the right provider for a condition as complex as autism was always going to be a process of trial and error, an integral part of the journey.

I spoke to Sophie and Tineke about starting a feeding program, and this time they finally agreed. After five months, they felt they knew Harry well enough to create something which had a chance of being successful. They had just undertaken some additional training on using ABA for avoidant restrictive food intake disorder or ARFID. Tineke warned it would be a slow process. Each food we wished to introduce would have to be run as its own target, but they would approach it as a desensitisation program, much like they had done with the shoes. I had radically accepted that food was going to be a lifelong battle for Harry. If we could get anywhere with it without harming him, that would be better than being right here.

I made an additional request to Tineke. If Harry really didn't like a food after trying it, I didn't want to persist with it. All I wanted was for him to give new foods a try and find out for himself if it was possible to like them. Tineke agreed. Research had shown that a person needed to try a new food at least twenty times to decide whether they liked it or not. That would be the aim, to introduce new foods with the goal of getting him to bite, chew and swallow it twenty times. If he got to that point and tolerated it, we would try to generalise the skill by providing that food in a home setting. If he did not like it, we would abandon it and try something else in its place.

We began the program with the careful selection of three foods. Two were foods he had previously eaten and dropped—an oat biscuit and grapes. If these could be attained, they would provide something to put in his lunchbox at kinder and school. The third was a new food—round-abouts—similar to a corn puff but shaped as a crispy halo, essentially a baby's first food. Sophie wanted to have something on the plate that would be an easy win, that he could be rewarded for so he would form positive associations with the new program. They started the program each day with a social story, personalised with photos of him and the family, and talking about how it was important to eat food to become big and strong like the Hulk. He sat for it and looked at each page as it was read to him. As with the shoe program, they started with a task so easy that even Harry couldn't believe he was being rewarded for it. He was asked to touch each of the three foods on the plate with his finger for one second. Once completed, he was given immediate access to his choice of a tub of Lego or a Captain America shield and that was the target done with for that session.

The levels were broken down to the smallest steps possible to ensure progress was gradual. Levels included giving the food a kiss, giving the food a lick, giving the food a chomp and spitting it out, giving the food a chomp and swallowing it. He often completed the program in character or had Bun-Bun sit next to him for a tea party. Almost all the time during the first year that the program was run, he required us to be seated next to him. It was a far more difficult program than the shoe program and he found astounding ways to delay and avoid it.

He usually had a milk and snack break halfway through the session and would call for it at exactly the moment when it was time for the food program, then claim to be too full to do the program after. He could see it coming up on the visual schedule. He came up with all kinds of conditions that needed to be satisfied before doing the program, such as for both Paul and me to be in the house, or for Paul to dial in on a video call from work to join him for the tea party.

One of his favourite tricks was to use ABA back upon the BTs. 'First you say *quack quack* and then I'll take a bite.' As frustrating as his procrastination was, he rarely got into a prolonged stand-off. Rather than wearing him down, this approach continued to draw out more of the imaginative and witty little boy. Progress was slow and whenever there was refusal, they dropped back and repeated the level before, but in this manner, after a month, he was eating the round-abouts. A week after that, he had the oat biscuit, but the grape increasingly disgusted him. He gagged and coughed. He would successfully complete the requested tasks for the other two foods and then escape from the room once it got to the grape.

By this point, he had generally become comfortable enough with the BTs that I could leave him in the designated therapy room and go to the kitchen to prepare dinner or spend a few minutes with Tessa. Often, he followed me around, forcing the BTs to follow him to the kitchen, or the study or wherever I was, and continue running the program, but at least he was no longer panicked that I had moved into a different location in the house. I was still unable to leave the house, but it was an improvement on the situation six months earlier. However, the grape saw all that progress undone and I found myself again required to sit in the therapy room the entire time until the food program was run. He hadn't quite got around to trying the grape twenty times, but I had seen enough to make the call to end it.

That was the fate of many of the items attempted on the food program over the next two years—sausages, vegetable fritters, raisin toast, butter sandwiches. But we had success, too—plain toast without even a scrape of butter, plain granola clusters, potato crisps and peeled slices of apple became mastered targets. It may sound pitiful for two years' worth of work, but they were easily accessible foods that gave us the ability to take the kids on short holidays and introduced a small amount of variety into his diet. It was success achieved without harming any of the relationships Harry had with the BTs, and in my eyes, the approach defined the key to Happy Oak's success with Harry.

Happy Oak not only customised his ABA program, they designed the entire program from scratch just for him. I had witnessed firsthand two programs built on the same ABA principles but packaged and delivered entirely differently. Happy Oak may not have attributed the label PDA to Harry's anxiety-based need for control, but they recognised it and honoured it. Tineke once said, 'We will do things a little bit on his terms and a little bit on ours. We can give him back some control.' They followed through with their requests and withheld rewards if he refused a task, but they took exceptional care in how they framed those requests in the first place. They committed to fanciful, indulgent and exhausting role play and they won him over.

I try not to think too much about where we might be today had we not found Happy Oak as our overall ABA provider first off. I do believe we would have kept trying until we found just the right people for Harry. His behaviour was unbearable and gave us no choice. But I can imagine the scale of the expectation and ensuing disappointment if it hadn't worked out the first time, and the temptation to just give up. The entire intake and rapport-building process was prolonged and expensive. Having to do it more than once would have been devastating. My only advice for families in this phase of their autism journey is to pursue each reasonable option with the kind of diligence and urgency that underpins the fact that time is of the essence, because the early years are golden, but to know that not everything may work out. Try anything, but do no harm.

TRICK OR TREAT

By the end of May 2021, the return to normal living conditions had seen virus numbers rise quickly again. The newly developed COVID-19 vaccines had been in the process of a phased rollout across Australia since March. Vaccinations were prioritised for older and vulnerable Australians, then progressively made available to the balance of the population, but uptake had been hesitant. The most readily available of the vaccines, AstraZeneca, had met with some bad press due to rare cases of blood clots as a possible side effect. Large numbers of the eligible community were holding out for the more limited Pfizer vaccine.

A vigorous anti-vaccination movement had gained momentum over the preceding months. It culminated in a fascinating meetup between the mistrust of science, anti-government sentiments and social media influence that saw a once-in-a-lifetime moment when members of the hippy-left got into bed with the conspiracy-theorising far-right to oppose the vaccine mandates that were being introduced to workers across all the states and territories in Australia.

On 28 May 2021, Victoria was hit with another snap lockdown, its fourth. It was intended to last seven days but eventually ran to fourteen. Stage Four restrictions returned with the same four reasons for leaving the home, and now the addition of a fifth—for eligible people to leave and get vaccinated against COVID-19. Remote learning was back. The five-kilometre radius was back, though this time playgrounds remained open. We had increased Harry's ABA to twenty hours a week, at his request. Having rotating batches of fresh adults to play with, he had discovered, was preferable to his tired and irritated parents.

'Who-one is coming to play with me today?' he would ask each morning.

Harry's demand avoidance of some of his daily tasks had lessened. A few of them, such as brushing his teeth or washing his hands, when prompted in creative ways, became fun for him. The veil of dysfunction that had been cloaking him started to lift. We caught glimpses here and there of a highly intelligent, imaginative and playful little boy. He remained extremely anxious and controlling, but he became increasingly accepting of the idea of reciprocity and cooperation. He was funny. My love for him had been unconditional from the day he was born, but for the first time I was finding him likeable, too.

I started to wonder whether Harry actually was PDA. I had read such adamant statements that strategies used for other autistic children, such as ABA, could not possibly work for children with PDA. By deduction, that meant since it was working, he must not have had PDA. These days, I have no doubt that he meets the PDA profile, but the statements had been propagated with such conviction. Espoused to an audience of vulnerable and broken parents, they were readily absorbed and repeated from one parent to another as fact. With my sample size of just one PDA child, I was no expert in ABA, PDA or autism. Perhaps if ABA had been applied in a generic, off-the-shelf manner, it would not have been effective for Harry, but applied in a highly customised, creative and flexible fashion, it was slowly but steadily having its desired effect.

I reflected on how many times I had seen parents on a PDA forum ask if anyone had tried ABA, or positive behaviour support, or some other ABA-based approach for their child, only for the same handful of voices to dogmatically and aggressively state that ABA or anything based on it was harmful and would not work. How absolute and lacking in nuance those words now sounded, yet at the time they had been powerful enough that I felt ashamed for even entertaining the idea of ABA. I wondered how many parents had been dissuaded from this path, had missed the opportunity that might have seen their child learn skills to dramatically improve his or her quality of life. ABA had painstakingly built a bridge that allowed Harry to connect with us, his family, and ultimately, with the rest of the world. As a result, it dramatically improved our lives, too.

The wellbeing of those caring for an autistic child is often perilously cast aside as an afterthought. In all the debate about ABA, very little of it turned upon how ABA might save the remaining members of the family, for example, by teaching fair sibling play skills or flexible thinking to accommodate others' needs. In the early days, the mammoth task we faced as the parents of an autistic child was crushing. We received so much expert advice but managed to convert so little of it into real solutions. The magnitude of the struggle we endured for each small amount of gain felt entirely hopeless. Harry monopolised so much of our time, there was none spare for attending to our own mental health. Yet, much more so than with a typical child, Harry's wellbeing depended heavily on Paul and me. Our ability to keep it together was no less important than Harry's. Given his high dependency, one of us falling apart would have been catastrophic for the rest of the family. ABA proved to be a lifeline for us, the parents. It provided us with experts who not only advised from a clinician's office but joined us in the trenches. Anyone who has ever been in the trenches will understand what that means.

Despite all the gains, Harry's ability to be independent, to do anything outside the home without holding my or Paul's or Big Tessa's hand had progressed little after seven months of ABA. In literal terms, this involved him holding my hand as he slid down a playground slide; partly because he feared the slide and partly because he feared the other children who were in close vicinity to the slide. Paul's parents had started coming over to babysit again but were now only useful for looking after Tessa or walking the dog. Harry unequivocally rejected them, particularly Paul's dad. He hadn't forgotten who they were, his memory was exceptional. There was no doubt he still recalled the excursions he had gone on with them previously, but they had lost their credibility as familiar, safe people and were required to rebuild rapport all over again. There were no credits awarded for previous time spent. It took over four months of consistent exposure before he was willing to play in the house with Pa again without Paul or me present.

My thoughts turned to kindergarten the following year. What had seemed an absolute impossibility months ago was now looking like a slight possibility, provided we could send a safe person along with him. I tried not to be too indulgent about thoughts of kinder, but the more I tried to resist it, the more incessant those thoughts became. I desperately wanted him to attend three-year-old kinder the following year, when he would, in fact, be four for most of the year. Harry was much better company than before, but he remained exhausting company and I longed for a break from him. I dreaded the thought of being tied down to him every moment of the day for another year, and I was going to do everything in my power to ensure I would not end up stuck in a home-schooling situation with him.

Paul wasn't volunteering for that role, either. He was adamant that Harry could go to kinder at a special school. Or he could have an integration aide. He could even go part time, but under no circumstances was he doing the same thing at home for another year. He was incredibly bright, and hungry for greater learning than I could offer him from the confines of our home, so much so I was sure it would drive us both to insanity to try. We never had his IQ tested. There didn't seem to be a need for it. He frequently outsmarted us, recalled things said to him verbatim, was incredibly perceptive to the most minor of details.

We called the local kindergarten a three-minute walk up our street and enquired about making special arrangements for a child on the spectrum for the following year. Specifically, we wanted to discuss whether Harry could attend with one of his BTs as an integration aide. Paul took Harry to meet with the director of the kindergarten in person and was stunned to be told they had never had a child use such an arrangement before, and that it would be harder for Harry to fit in with an aide. She had dealt with many anxious children over her twenty years of teaching and there was no approach quite like just ripping off the Band-Aid, she said. I bristled as Paul relayed the conversation to me. This was unexpected.

Under Victorian law, education providers, including kindergartens, were obliged to make reasonable adjustments to ensure that children with disabilities could take part in mainstream programs. Those education providers were eligible to apply for government funding for additional supports, for example, the employment of a teaching assistant. Since Harry would not just accept any adult allocated to him as a teaching assistant, by providing a BT as his aide, we were saving them the trouble of that paperwork. BTs worked in kinder and childcare settings frequently. I felt an immediate and fiery urge to argue his case, to force them to make allowances for him. If I hadn't strongly identified as part of the disability community before, I did now. This was the first time we had been denied special consideration since receiving Harry's diagnosis and I wanted nothing more than to teach them a lesson.

'We could just send Harry to the kinder for a day and watch them come begging us for an aide,' I said to Paul.

Paul was the voice of reason. He had pre-empted I would want to run up the street to take my case to the kindergarten director like a sledgehammer. But even if I flattened all the barriers and convinced the kinder to accept Harry with the supports and accommodations that we felt he needed, he didn't want Harry to be sent in as the guinea pig, to be the first one to housetrain the kinder for other kids on the spectrum.

'There are heaps of kinders around here,' he said. 'Let's just find one that has done this before.'

He was right. Harry was inflexible and this kinder was inflexible. We needed someone to be flexible.

I called around the kinders in our area and was instantly relieved to discover that all the rest of them would accommodate an aide. Most of them were, in fact, delighted at the idea of having an additional adult on the floor. We chose a small, cosy little kinder whose director was deeply apologetic for my initial experience and reassured me that they were very familiar with ABA and had worked with BTs in the past. They had a sensory room set aside that children could retreat to if they were overwhelmed or needed a break from the group activity.

'We would love to have the opportunity to teach Harry,' she said. 'The other children just love it when there's an extra adult around. They won't think anything of it.'

The kindness in her voice brought a lump to my throat. I had been gearing up for battle but now peacefully lay down my weapons. I had found a safe place for Harry next year and had six months left to prepare him for a positive first educational experience. Sophie had been thinking about kinder, too. She had the BTs introduce a new program involving me leaving the house for short periods of time. It was met with enormous and disproportionate resistance by Harry. I began with exceptionally small tasks taking less than a minute, such as stepping out of the front door to take the rubbish to the bins sitting five metres away in the driveway. I tried performing this task openly by announcing to him that I was putting out the rubbish, then I tried to do it discretely as if it were no big deal to step outside without warning for a few seconds. Either way, he screamed, abandoned whatever he was doing and immediately ran out after me, demanding that I not put out the rubbish, or that he put it out with me.

His intense opposition forced the therapists to alter the program so that it became Harry who left the house. He had a little more control as the leaver. It was a bit more familiar to him since he had been leaving the house with Big Tessa, but he still came up with a wild array of excuses to avoid it. It was too cold, too wet, too sunny. There were too many cockatoos outside, or not enough cockatoos. He wanted Roxy, our dog, to come. He only wanted to go outside if he was going to Sydney. Eventually, he would get to the doorstep only to say that he needed to bring his toys with him and go back inside to choose so many toys, spending so long choosing them, that either the time was up, or he was unable to carry them all. He was anxious and his demand avoidance was back, obliterating any doubts I had about PDA.

Eventually, over the next six months, he did go up and down the street to collect flowers and gumnuts. Progression wasn't linear. There were many days when he refused to go, but over time he progressed, such that towards the end of the year, he managed the five-minute walk down to the local playground, sometimes dressed in a full Hulk costume including the mask. Once there, he had such an enjoyable time that he was often reluctant to leave, causing the BTs to call me for assistance to get him back for dinner.

As his sense of independence grew, I saw the opportunity to again test out his tolerance for me leaving the house. I had observed that Paul or me leaving abruptly invariably resulted in a furious and panicked protest. It was a source of recurring frustration for me that Paul picked the worst times to head out the door for a run, slamming the door loudly with his headphones on and sprinting off down the street, oblivious to the wails and screams he left behind, or perhaps because of it. It didn't matter that the BT and I were still there. Harry had three adults in the house, and he just lost control of one of them.

I used my cunning.

'Oh, Harry, I just got a message to say one of your new toys has arrived at the post office. You can get it as a reward today! You can't come though, COVID rules. One person only! I'll be a few minutes!'

It wasn't a question. It was a grand statement that I was off to do him a favour. I put on my shoes, smiled brightly and walked out the door with false confidence. It worked. I came back ten minutes later to a calm Harry who came to the door smiling with anticipation.

'What is it? Did you get it?'

I began leaving the house briefly but regularly, fabricating the kinds of creative excuses that Harry would have been proud to come up with. Some days it didn't work. If I picked the wrong time to attempt my departure, for example, just as he was about to do the food program, or some other non-preferred task that had already heightened his anxiety, I dashed the opportunity for that session and was commanded to sit with him for the remainder of the time so he could keep tabs on me. But, with persistence, I did eventually get to a point where I could leave long enough to complete a grocery run.

16 July 2021 saw another five-day lockdown, the fifth, imposed in response to an outbreak of the new Delta strain of the virus which was traced back to interstate removalists coming from Sydney to deliver furniture into Melbourne. Stage Four restrictions were back. These snap lockdowns were part of a strategy to keep infections controlled until seventy per cent of the population were fully vaccinated, meaning two doses of the vaccine. They were announced in the morning and commenced at midnight the same day, marketed as pocket-sized gloom and doled out with the hope of staving off prolonged suffering. Again, the lockdown was extended by another week to 27 July.

We emerged from that lockdown for nine days only to go back in on 5 August 2021 for one last round. The number of cases was just six, but those cases had been active in the community and the exposure sites included schools and supermarkets. It was announced as a seven-day snap lockdown and this time it took effect at 8.00 pm that night, just a few hours after its announcement that afternoon. The community collectively clutched their heads. A few hundred people took to the city streets in violent protests. Lockdowns had become 2021's recurring nightmare for five million Melburnians. Even with government financial support, hundreds of businesses were unable to survive the two years of repeated lockdowns. People lost their jobs. Casual workers and those in insecure or low-income jobs were particularly affected with many not eligible for government lockdown payments.

I, however, was in a far better position to handle the 2021 lockdowns compared to the ones in the year before, and even in the midst of them, that fact was not lost on me. Life was invariably harder in lockdown. The kids fought more within the confines of the home, and the monotony was stifling. But relative to other people, our lives in lockdown weren't that much worse than how we lived outside of it. I had two children who were too young to need home-schooling. As an existing ABA client, Harry was permitted to continue his therapy largely uninterrupted, so the BTs kept him occupied for a few hours each day, five days a week. Yes, I sat in the room with him, but I had been doing that all year and now everyone else had joined me in doing virtually the same thing, except that they were probably trying to work remotely as well. My fear of missing out was turned down to the minimum it had been in years. The world wasn't moving forward, and I wasn't being left behind. A perverse sense of satisfaction crept up on me now that everyone else was wallowing in the same swamp of misery.

The sixth lockdown didn't end in seven days. Nor did it end after another seven-day extension. Melbourne was fatiguing under the cumulative effect of two years under house arrest. Parties and gatherings were held in contravention of the rules. Case numbers rose sharply and on 16 August, the restrictions tightened and a curfew was reintroduced. By the end of the month, case numbers were in the seventies. A month after that, they were in the 700s. The horse had truly bolted, and the city knew it was not getting out of lockdown by suppressing the case numbers. We were in for an extended lockdown until the threshold seventy-per-cent vaccination rate was reached.

Time was no longer defined by hours or days or even weeks. It existed in lumps, large and shapeless, and when cut, glooped back together and merged into one. My recollections of how we passed our time those last two lockdowns are vague. They weren't bad enough to be seared into my memory and I have few photos from those months since the sameness of the situation from one day to the next didn't warrant capturing any.

At one point, Tessa developed a high temperature that persisted for days. We suspected a urinary tract infection, which it ultimately was, but she was not toilet trained and we were unable to catch a urine sample. A pandemic was a bad time to be visiting an emergency department, but she remained so unwell that I reluctantly took her to the Royal Children's Hospital. I spent close to ten hours there with her as we waited in a long queue for her urine to be sampled using a catheter. It was an ordeal which I had originally presented to Tessa as an outing to meet some doctors at the aquarium. There was an impressive two-storey fish tank in the emergency waiting area at the hospital that housed exotic fish, including a huge lumpy Maori Wrasse. Tessa had watched Finding Nemo but had not yet visited an actual aquarium. As far as she knew, this was it.

I attended a virtual drinks night on Zoom one evening with my university friends, some of whom I hadn't seen for close to two years. Nearly all of them had turned forty at some point over the two years of lockdowns. What should have been a time of plentiful glittering parties was instead reduced to one online meeting of ten women in sweaters or pyjamas trying to shoo away children breaching their bedtime.

The kids rode their bikes on training wheels and visited playgrounds which mercifully remained open as a small gesture of grace for the sixth lockdown. We indulged them with the odd evening walk to gaze up at the stars. One particularly brilliant moonlit night, we wandered down our street with Roxy, our docile old dog following a few steps behind, to admire the vista of a radiant full moon that was seemingly suspended just above the treetops at the end of our street. It highlighted every detail of suburban life under the wash of its silver light. The children had seen the moon depicted in story books and on the television, but this was their first sighting of it for real.

'Tessa! Let's howl,' cried Harry. He must have, of course, come across a video on YouTube involving werewolves and full moons.

'How?'

'Howl!'

'How?'

Seeing his sister's confusion, Harry turned his face towards the moon, drew in a deep breath and dramatically unleashed a long, bloodcurdling howl into the cool night air, the wisps of steam from his breath adding to the dramatic effect.

'Ahwoooooo,' his voice rang out down the street.

Tessa cackled with glee, then joined in. Roxy's ears flicked back and forth. She was a sweet old thing. She took a few steps back with uncertainty and sought safety behind a tree from where she continued to watch her human siblings stand side by side, facing the moon, howling their lungs out.

Paul grew his whiskey collection. I put up the fingerboard and did a few minutes of training each day. We waited for the population to get vaccinated. Full vaccination initially meant two doses of a COVID-19 vaccine twelve weeks apart, but the guidelines were later shortened to anytime between eight to twelve weeks to speed up the process.

It would be 21 October 2021 by the time the seventy-per-cent double vaccination threshold was reached, putting an end to the lockdown with a promise there would be no more. The residents of Melbourne had spent 245 days under stay-at-home orders, earning them the ignominious title of being the world's most locked-down city. In the week leading up to this, there were signs of hope visible in our neighbourhood. Halloween was approaching. In previous years, a smattering of houses in each neighbourhood observed this American tradition, but that year, families with young children bored out of their minds for months on end had started decorating their houses early in anticipation, elaborately and excessively, taking great care to create frightening scenes. Tessa cried when she first saw the house at the end our street completely transformed by a thick net of cobwebs over the entire fence, a gigantic spider with legs bristling with coarse hairs sitting guard on one side of the entrance, a corpse on the other. Harry ran up to it. We already knew about his love of villains, but now we had just stumbled upon his penchant for the haunted and ghoulish.

Except for the Hulk, his interest in the Avengers had waned and I had struggled for months to find motivating reinforcers for ABA therapy. With shops now open again, my weekly schedule included at least one trip to an op shop so that I could drop off the extraordinary number of toys that were no longer interesting, only to pick up another assorted load to take home. Suddenly, I was gifted with a new special interest and knickknacks were in season and in plentiful supply.

He wanted nothing more for a reward than a new Halloween decoration to hang up around the house. He liked the cute ones—the smiling ghosts and pumpkins—just as much as he liked the genuinely terrifying ones—the zombies and skeletons. I had never seen him so compliant, diligent, hurried even, to complete his ABA targets. He wanted to leave the house with the BTs, to go for walks and admire the decorations at other houses. He wanted me to leave the house to go to the shops and find more Halloween trinkets. We carved a pumpkin and then we carved an even better pineapple. I had never done Halloween before, but that year I was all in.

On 30 October, lockdown behind us, we joined the hoards that went trick-or-treating. Tessa had gotten used to the scenes of horror lining our streets and she was happily dressed as a gorgeous little tutu-clad witch clutching a pumpkin basket. It blew her mind that today she was actually being encouraged to walk up to people's houses, ring the doorbell and have someone come out to put candy in her basket. It was the best day of her life. Harry was dressed as the Hulk, an excellent one, with rippling muscles and torn purple pants and a fearsome expression on his mask. Everywhere he went, people greeted him as the Hulk. He nodded back in acknowledgement, safe from behind his mask.

Initially, he was hesitant about approaching the doors, stopping halfway up the path and looking back towards us, waiting for Paul or me to take his hand. But after the first few houses, he was emboldened by Tessa who enthusiastically shouted, 'trick-or-treat' and took her candy with a sweet, 'tank you'. He began walking up to the door and standing close behind Tessa, no longer needing our hand. Soon he ran up to the door, desperate to be the first to ring the doorbell or knock. Eventually, he said, 'trick-or-treat', too.

So keen were the children of Melbourne to go trick-or-treating that many houses ran out of candy after half an hour. Harry, who had collected a basketful, didn't eat candy or chocolate and he began emptying the contents of his basket back into the empty bowls of the houses he visited, much to the confused delight of other children. We got back home after over an hour of trick or treating. It had been warm. The Hulk costume was hot to wear, the mask was too big for his face and partially obstructed his sight, but Harry had not complained once. He had walked under his own power without being carried and at no stage did he threaten a meltdown. For the first time outside our house, in a sustained manner, he had acted independently of us. It was a momentous outing. He was tired, but despite not eating any of his loot, he was completely sated.

I turned forty in November and was eligible to have a party, but freshly out of hibernation and still shrouded by a lack of having something to look forward to, I was far from being in the mood for a party. I was still towing around an assorted trailer of melancholy and ill temper. I was an introvert who had successfully learnt the skills to disguise it in my twenties. It had paid dividends at work to pretend that I was not one, and I had become exceptionally honed at it, but those skills had fallen out of practice. It was like returning to exercise after a long hiatus. My social muscles had atrophied. I was relieved the monotony was over but on the other side of it, I was equally fatigued by sustained in-person interactions.

Adding to my lacklustre levels of enthusiasm was the fact that lockdown had finished, but our lives had not significantly improved. My days continued to be spent at home with Harry in therapy, much as they had been during lockdown. It was dead time. It didn't require my full attention, but I also wasn't in a position to get a side project underway. On bad days, I wasn't allowed to leave the therapy room, and on good days, Harry could still successfully thwart my attempts to cook a simple dinner.

I could see other families heading off to beach houses or going interstate for holidays, but we were still effectively locked down by Harry's routine which imposed an approximate limit of thirty minutes from home. We couldn't eat dinner at a restaurant since we needed Harry's exact brand of chicken tenders. We needed quick access to multiple changes of clothing in case a drop of water fell from his drink bottle. With little notice, he could suddenly and intensely develop the idea that he needed a very particular toy from home. I refused to acknowledge my fortieth birthday other than by breaking up a fight between Harry and Tessa as they scuffled with one another to blow out a candle on a little birthday cake. The candle was eventually lit seven times, with Harry blowing it out the first six.

Paul raced out to go fly-fishing, heading to the Gippsland rivers for a much-needed break. Then he started meeting friends for dinner. He, too, was struggling to process the disparity between our lives and others. He found it hard to make small talk and casual banter, but his desire to engage and be among peers was stronger than mine. He got more back from the effort he put in to be in their company. I was resentful that he bothered to go out at all. How was he not as miserable as me? Did he really think he could resurrect his former life? What was there to enjoy about hanging out with people who offered trite sympathy through comments like, 'Oh, I know! Tommy is such a picky eater too!'? I couldn't handle it. I built a fortress and shut myself in.

Faced with the widening gulf between us, Paul did the one thing he knew might bring me some joy. He organised for Chad to go on a birthday climb with me and we headed out to the Cathedral Ranges. It was under two hours from Melbourne but with its rugged ridgelines, challenging approach and prickle bushes that guarded access to the remnants of this old volcano, I felt I had escaped my reality much farther.

We chose a mid-grade climb of three pitches, and alternated leads. The protection on this route was solid but sparse in many places. I knew that because the guidebook had made a point of it, noting that the route had been the site of some very long falls. I had embarked upon the climb fully expecting unease to overtake me like the last time we were outdoors. Yet, with my toes perched lightly on a delicate foothold on the slabby buttress, I was neither panicked nor worried. I moved cautiously but wasted no time searching for protection in places where I could see that none was available. I led onwards and glanced down to see five metres of unprotected rope swaying gently against the coarse sandstone. I moved with calm intent until I finally reached a flake that accepted gear. It was glorious, the risk titillating. I embraced it and for a few hours, I was no longer the mother of two, or the champion of an autistic boy.

'What do you actually do all day?' asked Chad earnestly, as we perched unevenly on the cramped belay ledge, a lumpy pile of climbing rope and a bunch of metal hardware pushing against our backsides.

Chad, hilariously, had no filter. I had climbed with him for a decade and had fielded a bunch of uncensored questions that ran through his head and came directly out of his mouth. It was fitting that he was the first person to ask me the question everyone else had avoided.

It was hard to account for my time, but given the opportunity, I found myself desperately wanting to. I tried my best to describe the hours each day spent at home with Harry in ABA, where my job was to interact as little as possible yet be visibly present to assuage his anxiety. I described how "going to the supermarket" actually involved going to three supermarkets to successfully fulfil our outrageously specific shopping list, and how getting him dressed might involve a hairdryer to dry an item of clothing that had been through the wash the day before that he really needed to wear again. I wanted to justify my own existence, my lack of employment, and why, once an abundance of potential, I had been laid to waste.

WHEN HARRY POTTER SAVED THE YEAR

'Hey, Harry,' I said tentatively. 'Big Tessa is supposed to go with you to kinder tomorrow, but she's got COVID and can't go. None of your teachers can fill in.'

'Then you come with me,' was his hopeful suggestion.

It was a suggestion that came out at every possible opportunity.

'Oh, I'm not allowed. Only teachers can go with you to kinder. They are the rules. You only get to have Big Tessa because she is studying to be a teacher.'

In 2022, Harry started doing three-year-old kindergarten two days a week. He turned four a month later and was the oldest in the class, but for the first six months he only did three hours each day and had an aide with him the entire time. We had made arrangements for one of his BTs or Big Tessa to attend with him. BTs frequently visited kindergartens or schools to teach children the skills necessary in those settings, but Harry was unique in requiring his own familiar person the entire time he was there to keep his anxiety at bay.

Paul and I had decided Harry could have his special person at all times at kinder, but under no circumstances could that person be one of us. His behaviour was significantly less controlling when he was accompanied by the BTs or Big Tessa, but mainly, we just didn't want the thought creeping into his head that it was a possibility one of us could be in attendance with him in an educational setting. We feared we would never be able to reverse the idea. Schooling was my ticket to freedom ... one day.

I had decided not to attempt working in 2022 or 2023, Harry's two years of kindergarten. The situation was too tenuous for me to be a reliable employee, and I was still traumatised by the memories of my last job. I flinched, recalling the feeling of being a disappointment and of failing to meet my own expectations. Harry only attended two days of kindergarten in the first year, and three days the following year, both on reduced hours, to accommodate his anxiety and his one-on-one ABA sessions. The greatest gains from ABA were to be had in the pre-school years, so we doubled down and put everything we had into it. He was now engaged in twenty-three hours of ABA each week, inclusive of the time spent at kinder with a BT.

With this part-time approach, kinder had started tentatively but smoothly. We had met with the kinder teacher and the kinder director in advance, briefed them on Harry's therapy goals and given them some strategies to help keep him calm and engaged. We urged them to be guided by Big Tessa and his BTs on how to manage him. They accepted all our suggestions. They encouraged and invited him to be involved, went along with his role play but never pushed too hard. He participated in some activities and chose to stand back and just watch for others. Sand and paint had become new sensory aversions, and he fervently avoided those. He had a particular dislike for standing in a circle and singing songs or performing prescribed actions in unison. At those times, he retreated with Big Tessa or the BTs to the sensory room to read a book or play with other toys.

When I came to pick him up halfway through the day, I watched him for a few minutes through a window. At the beginning of the year, Harry was often separated from the other children or engaged in a different activity from the others with his BT or Big Tessa. It looked like nothing more than he preferred to be doing something else. I was not disappointed. I was just relieved he wasn't crying, and I thought, *that's my boy, he's autistic and he likes to do his own thing, he prefers to play with adults.* Over the course of the next two years, this slowly changed. At first, without realising the significance of what I was seeing, from my spot at the window I watched as he became increasingly integrated with the rest of the kindergarten group. I would go to pick him up halfway through the day to find him running trains along a track he had built with some other children or sitting side by side with his best friend sharing a box of craft materials for a piece of artwork. One day, I looked through the window to see no children sitting inside, not even Harry. They were all running around the garden out the back. Harry was fully invested in a dinosaur fight with three other boys. In fact, he was providing direction to the others on what to play out next.

'No, you are Stegosaurus, so you are down here eating the leaves. Tommy is Pterodactyl. He is going to swoop down on you!'

The creativity and drama in role play that he displayed with unbridled enthusiasm at home was taking place in the kindergarten playground. He had finally gotten up the confidence to set himself free outside of the home.

Over the early years of our autism journey, I heard occasional words to the effect that kids with autism prefer to do their own thing rather than engage in play with other children. I do not doubt there are many who do hold such a preference, and it seemed also to fit in with my initial observations about Harry. However, with the fullness of time, I came to understand that what I first saw was a child who didn't necessarily want to play on his own, but a child who lacked the intuition and skills to play with others. He had the defensive skills to make it look like he would rather be doing something on his own, and he made sure he was always consumed by something else. Skills of engagement that came so naturally to Tessa had to be taught to Harry in a step-by-step fashion, but once learnt, he was highly motivated to use them to access a world of unlimited play with other children.

He didn't like to outright admit to me that he was enjoying kinder. He seemed to delight in watching me jump through hoops each day to get him there. When I asked if he had had a good day, he would reply with a restrained, 'Uh-huh'. But I could tell from the amount of thought he placed into selecting which toys to bring with him each day to show his friends that he had, in fact, grown fond of kinder and his little friends there.

In July 2022, one of the major supermarkets released a new promotional campaign featuring collectable Harry Potter figures that could be built from little cardboard pop-outs and were rather adorable. Harry loved collectables and these were plastic-free. Finally, there was something that could be collected at the checkout that wouldn't make me hate myself a little bit each time. Suddenly, twenty years behind the trend, I was very interested in Harry Potter. From the moment I got my head around the main characters, I knew this would be the greatest special interest so far in Harry's life.

I carefully planted the seed by showing Harry a few little snippets of the movies, selling it as part of his Halloween obsession, which was still very much ongoing nine months later. Next, I offered a few of the buildable Harry Potter figures. He had a fantastical mind and it had been waiting to grasp onto its next special interest. It took little effort for him to fall head over heels into J. K. Rowling's dizzying, colourful, opulent world of magic and wizardry.

'Tomorrow, everyone is going to kinder dressed up as their favourite hero,' I reminded Harry.

We had bought him Harry Potter's number seven quidditch robe for the occasion. It went well with the replica Nimbus 2000 racing broomstick he had earned as a reward a few weeks earlier. He had been excited about dressing up as Harry Potter, but with the knowledge that Big Tessa wasn't going to be there, he was wavering. He had never started a kinder day on his own before. We had tried having the BTs run late. They hid up the street in their cars as I attempted to drop off Harry at the door with all the other children, promising him they would meet him inside a few minutes later, but it never worked.

After two terms at kinder, we had started extending his stay into the afternoon, after the BTs left for the morning. He eventually managed to complete the afternoon hours on his own. The first few times were just for fifteen minutes, and he knew upfront that would be the case. Nevertheless, when the moment came, there were tears and panic with the kinder teachers needing to physically restrain him at the door to stop him from running out down the pathway after his BT. After weeks, he had eventually been able to accept the situation with the offer of extravagant Harry Potter themed rewards such as the broomstick, a plush Hedwig the owl in a cage, replica wands belonging to the various characters. The patient and kind teachers had arranged for one of them to be in close proximity to him at all times, and finally he managed to stay the remaining three hours on his own without being distressed.

Walking into kinder solo had until that point remained an insurmountable challenge. He flatly refused to step past the doorway without his special adult. That day, I detected an opportunity. Where he would previously have cried out a distressed, 'No! I'm not going to kinder!', he instead remained silent, deep in thought. This was the closest thing to a yes I could have hoped for. I had to make it happen.

'Just fly into kinder on your broomstick. I'll even find you a golden snitch to chase after and catch,' I said, referring to one of the three types of balls used in the wizard sport of quidditch.

I had a golden snitch hidden away. It had been an old Christmas tree decoration I had found at an op shop, but it was just the right size, shiny with golden wings. I had been saving it for a moment just like this. A smile broke out on his face. He had an incredibly vivid imagination and what I was saying must have played out as a pretty exciting scene in his head.

'Okay! If you get a golden snitch, I will go, but I get to keep the golden snitch as a reward!'

We had a deal.

The next morning, we dressed him in quidditch robes, drew a lightening scar on his forehead and put on his Harry Potter glasses. He tucked a wand into his robe, took his broomstick in one hand and held a birdcage with Hedwig in it in the other. He looked at himself in the mirror and smiled proudly at me, dimples ablaze. I sent a silent thanks to J. K. Rowling for all the ornate details and embellishments of her stories. I was exploiting every one of them to blend fantasy with reality for Harry and he was slowly inching closer to independence at kinder.

'Where's the golden snitch?' he asked, as I parked the car in front of the kinder.

He clambered out slowly, starting to procrastinate, fussing around with how to hold his broomstick and his birdcage. Much like with the shoes, I knew I had to stop him from having the time to let doubt set in. I grabbed his backpack and the golden snitch and jumped in front of him, holding it before his eyes.

'I want a nice fair game,' I called out, before dashing down the footpath, leaving the car door wide open as it was. I didn't have any time to waste.

Harry mounted his broomstick and ran after me. I held the golden snitch and ran erratically, slaloming down the street towards the kinder. He followed. Then he improvised, adding his own touch to the drama.

'Oh no! My broom is broken!' he cried as he dramatically held onto his bucking broomstick before it sideswiped a bush.

Other parents stood aside to let us through, bemused by the whir of energy at that time of morning. They knew Harry well and some yelled words of encouragement, realising what was happening.

'Get the snitch, Harry, win the game for Gryffindor,' someone yelled.

I got to the first child-safety gate marking entry onto the kinder grounds.

'Quick, Harry, get your wand! Unlock the gate!'

'Alohomora!' he yelled without hesitation, reciting the incantation used for opening locked doors.

I unlocked the gate and flung it open. I continued to move fast and theatrically. I had to keep the energy levels up so that he only had time to think and not to feel. We arrived at the door and were greeted by his teacher who had dressed up as the Easter bunny. He was now met with other children dressed up as Elsa from Frozen and Fireman Sam. He didn't just like his own fantasy world, he liked other people's, too. His teacher took a cue from me and hustled him inside immediately. I made the sign of a telephone with my hand and put it up to my ear once Harry had his back to me. *Call me if this doesn't work out.* She nodded.

I didn't get a call that day. I picked him up at 3.00 pm with everyone else. He rode his broomstick out the door, smiling. It was the story of his life. Resistance, struggle, one form of role play after another, and sometimes a breakthrough. Walking into kinder unaccompanied each day didn't follow on seamlessly after that, but it did occur haphazardly, and then more frequently, until in the last few weeks of the year, it became the norm that his BT would arrive half an hour after him.

We rode off Harry Potter's robe tails for the better part of two years, and to this day, all the books and films remain a formidable motivating force whenever we are faced with a challenging behaviour requiring modification. One of the most intimidating tasks we faced was toilet training Harry. We had made two previous attempts to toilet train him in the preceding twelve months. We read children's stories about pooping in the toilet and watched social stories on YouTube. We offered handsome rewards but found no success. Harry hung stubbornly and anxiously onto his usual pooping routine, which I had helped to reinforce over the past year.

It was only in his Harry Potter era that I saw a real potential to get this now four-year-old toddler out of his nappies. On Facebook Marketplace, I had joined a Harry Potter collectibles buy-and-sell group and someone was selling a Sorting Hat. It was an excellent replica that could be worn on the head, and which muttered its own musings through a moving mouth before calling out one of the four houses that all new students to the Hogwarts School of Witchcraft and Wizardry got sorted into. Even for Harry, who was used to being indulged with all sorts of high-performing toys, this one was truly in a class of its own. I bought it and when I collected it, I held it in both hands and pressed my forehead gently against its soft, wrinkled fabric, willing it with every iota of telepathy I possessed to please be successful as the great poop reward.

It was a fortunate confluence of opportunities when Tessa, who forever wanted to be a big girl, became highly motivated to be toilet trained at around the same time. We began a competitive process, something I had been loath to do up until that point, of pitting one child directly against the other in a race to see who could get toilet trained first, which they both accomplished at roughly the same time. Tessa got some butterfly wings and Harry got his Sorting Hat, which, to his great delight, put him into the same house as Harry Potter—Gryffindor.

At the end of 2022, Harry performed in his kinder Christmas concert—singing along with the rest of his class and doing the set actions—a task he had resisted up until early November. He liked Santa and he liked Christmas. Just as with Halloween, he was fully invested in the festivity. He wanted me to come along to watch the concert, yet for weeks at pickup his teacher would say that, although he had had a great day, he was not willing to sing or do the actions, only to stand next to the rest of the group. She hadn't wanted to make him do anything he wasn't willing to, and I didn't want him to be forced either. But having learnt a lesson from watching him gradually begin playing with other children, I thought to ask him what the issue was.

He was quite articulate in his speech by then, able to make subtle distinctions between concepts and emotions. I asked him why he didn't want to sing along and do the actions with the rest of the group.

'Because I'm worried I might sing the wrong song,' he said in a matter-of-fact tone.

He was always the perfectionist, watching and withholding until he was utterly sure he had it right. But he was four years old, and it was not possible for him to get all seven songs in the concert and their actions completely right.

'Can you just sing quietly?' I suggested. 'There are fourteen other kids singing. I bet you Cooper is a loud singer! If you just sing quietly, no one will hear you over the sound of Cooper, even if you get the words wrong. I bet you Cooper will get some of the words wrong.'

I paused and looked at him. He was looking down at the floor but seemed to be thinking about my suggestion, so I continued.

'Everyone is just going to be moving their mouths and no one watching will be able to tell what noise is coming out of whose mouth, anyway.'

'Maybe,' he finally said.

'And I'm sure the teachers are doing the actions, too. Maybe you can watch them and follow along. If you're doing some actions, it's going to look less obvious than if you do no actions, even if they are wrong.'

He remained silent, but he was looking at me now.

'If you promise to sing along quietly and try to follow your teachers' actions, then I promise to come and watch.'

'Okay. I can try,' he said.

We had another deal, and on the day, we both held up our end of it. He was blank-faced, as he often was when overwhelmed by a situation, and he looked a bit stressed. His body was turned entirely sideways towards his teachers at the edge of the stage, intently following their actions, but he did it and was proud of himself, and I of him.

He had participated in something which he had secretly wanted to do but had been so anxious about that he had resisted it with the kind of totality that made everyone think he didn't want to be a part of it. I had learnt an important lesson—to not make assumptions about why Harry did or didn't do things. His mind sometimes worked differently to what I had learnt about human behaviour through forty years of existence. He sometimes gave off different cues to what one might expect, but unless he told me otherwise, I wouldn't be doing any favours by shielding him from the challenges, the opportunities and ultimately, the joys that every child needed to experience.

THE NUN

In 2022, Tessa went to childcare. Having her out of the house made running Harry's therapy much easier. After a short period of adjustment, it became patently clear just how naturally skilled Tessa was in the art of human relations. She had friends who rushed to greet her at the door. She joined or initiated play with complete mastery and took great joy in singing and dancing with the group. She got into altercations and got herself out of them. She was kind and helpful when other children were upset, and she welcomed comfort from others when she was.

I grew up as an only child with a stunted emotional development which I learnt to compensate for over time through observation and cognitive ability. I didn't suffer from a lack of emotions, nor a lack of insight into them, but I did have a severe absence of the skills needed to let them out functionally, particularly at crucial times. Emotions were never talked about with my parents, and in my adulthood, I struggled to convert them into words. I marvelled at Tessa the day she came home from childcare, age three, and said, 'Mama, I feel sad because Katy told me off for not packing up.' She was inviting me to console and counsel her about something I wouldn't have otherwise known about.

One of Tessa's friends at childcare went on a holiday and when she returned, she brought Tessa back a souvenir.

'Amy went on a plane to Queensland,' she said. 'I want to go on a plane, too.'

Paul and I had talked about taking the kids on a holiday. After all, we had each travelled widely and wildly in our twenties and thirties and spent countless hours over lockdown tempting ourselves with unrealistic holiday destinations on Instagram. Each time we had talked about a holiday, we had dismissed it as an impossibility. Harry's rigidity and routines, and his inability to eat the foods that were available in transit, ruled it out. Harry seemed perfectly satisfied with staying indoors and playing with toys. He didn't like the beach. He didn't want to get his hair wet. He detested putting on sunscreen. He got disgruntled about things easily and demanded to be carried.

Tessa and Harry were yin and yang. Tessa rubbed sunscreen on herself for fun, even when she wasn't going outside. She was a natural in the water. From age two and a half, she showed a great interest in diving underwater to pick up sinkable toys, able to hold her breath for longer than me. She was relaxed and playful. Tessa didn't require strict routines to keep her on track but went along with Harry's anyway. She wanted to go wherever anyone was going. I grimaced at the thought that she was missing out on fun because of Harry's inflexibility. Fun hadn't been a feature of my childhood, and I didn't want her to have the kind of relationship with me that I now had with my mum.

I broached a subject that had been raised and shot down before.

'Let's take them away to stay somewhere for just one night, no more than two hours' drive.'

Paul was intolerant of the chaos that emanated from the backseat of the car every time we took the kids anywhere, which admittedly had never exceeded forty-five minutes. They played loudly or argued, but either way it always sounded like a fight, and invariably it always ended up in a fight. One child's toy wrongfully touched the other child's toy, or a crumb from Tessa's snack rolled over onto Harry's side of the car, violating his space. Without fail, within twenty minutes there was bedlam.

'Maybe we can time the trip so that they fall asleep on the drive there.'

Paul was quiet. He'd had a happy childhood. He was probably flicking through his catalogue of memories of all the holidays with his sister, the road trips they had gone on as a family.

'Just one night. How bad can it be if Harry doesn't eat or sleep for one night?'

He agreed, not so much using words but through the reluctant act of pulling out his laptop to search for destinations under two hours from Melbourne.

We chose to stay for one night in Ballarat, near the tourist attraction of Sovereign Hill, a meticulously recreated 1850s gold mining town. It was an open-air museum representing life during Victoria's gold rush era and I still held good memories of a year four school camp there, panning for gold and practising cursive handwriting with chalk in a classroom. We chose an apartment with an oven so we could cook Harry's chicken tenders, and we packed colouring books and iPads to keep the kids occupied for the one-and-a-half-hour car ride, even though we were sure they would fall asleep.

They didn't fall asleep and shortly before we entered the highway, they had broken out into a raucous argument because Tessa had placed her plush toys in the middle seat in between their two child seats, a space that Harry considered neutral and could not be occupied by anyone or their toys. Tessa, on the other hand, was aggrieved that Harry had let out an almighty sneeze accompanied by droplets that sprayed onto her and refused to apologise. I ended up sitting between the two of them as peacekeeper, askew in the marginally sized middle seat, for the remaining hour of the journey. I let Harry watch some videos of his favourite YouTubers on the iPad. He was still deep into the Halloween theme and over the past few days had been repeatedly watching a skit made by some kids depicting a spooky evil nun based loosely on the horror film *The Conjuring*.

'I want to see a nun,' Harry declared when we got out of the car at Lake Wendouree in Ballarat.

We had an hour before we could check into the apartment and had stopped by the lake and adjoining botanical gardens. Tessa ran out to see the swans and ducks that waddled around on the banks. Harry hung around the car, oblivious to the idyllic scenes before us, as if waiting for me to produce a nun from behind the tree.

'Maybe there will be a nun going for a walk around the lake,' I suggested.

He would forget about the nun soon. We just had to move him onto something else. He followed us, a distance behind, grumbling. He wasn't interested in the sights on offer unless it involved a nun. We approached Paul and Tessa who had found their way to an excellent playground complete with mazes and turrets and slides evoking all kinds of medieval feels. It was the kind of playground Harry would normally love, but not today. He stood to one side, refusing to engage with any of the equipment on offer.

'I can't see a nun. I don't think they come to the playgrounds. Will there be one at the house where we are staying?'

Paul and I exchanged knowing glances. This nun thing perhaps wasn't going away anytime soon and was showing some potential for derailing the entire trip if we didn't manage to source one.

We checked into our apartment. We were in luck. Our apartment was within a heritage listed mansion built in 1901, and luxuriously renovated to feature magnificent chandeliers, a grand staircase, high ceilings and Victorian era décor.

'Wow!' both kids exclaimed with awe as we stepped into the building.

In the apartment, there was a bedroom for each child, and they set about arranging their rooms with the stash of toys they had each brought along. Then they played hide and seek in the various nooks and, unfortunately for other guests there, the apartment door did not lock from the inside, so they took their adventures to the hallways in the remainder of the mansion.

'Let's stay here forever!' shouted Tessa.

We breathed a sigh of relief. Harry had forgotten about the nun.

Later that day, as we ordered some takeaway and put Harry's chicken into the oven, we made the grave mistake of giving the kids their iPads while we waited for dinner and suddenly Harry was reminded of the nun.

'When am I going to see a nun?'

'What's a nun?' asked Tessa.

'Is there a nun in this house?' Harry continued. His voice was pressingly urgent.

'What's a nun?'

'Will there be a nun at Sovereign Hill tomorrow? If there isn't a nun, I don't want to go!'

'What's a nun?'

When Harry's special interest areas came on, they were obsessive, relentless and unyielding. They could not wait for a later time or place, nor did they make way for other things of interest. I can only imagine that for Harry they itched like a rash that could not be ignored and yet once scratched became more intense still. I had noticed that a cathedral was conveniently situated on the block adjacent to the mansion we were in.

'Harry, there is a big church behind this apartment. If you have a good dinner and drink all your smoothie, we can take a walk there and see if we can find a nun.'

I didn't like our chances. It was fast turning to night, but I just needed to buy enough patience from him to at least get through dinner.

At 6.30 pm, we rugged up for the cool autumn night, put on our beanies and took a walk to the cathedral. Tessa had never gone for a walk in the dark before, so this was an adventure. She squealed with excitement at the evening excursion as she rode atop Paul's shoulders. Her smile made me smile. I was glad we had taken them here to create memories of their first holiday together, even though my prevailing memory of the trip would be that we were wandering around on a Saturday night looking for nuns.

We arrived at the cathedral grounds. Tessa marvelled at its majestic architecture. Harry paid no attention to its beauty and began repeatedly asking how we could get in and whether the nuns were inside. I had just assumed it would remain open day and night lest someone found the urge to pray outside business hours. I thought we would have at least been able to go inside to have a look, perhaps seen some traces of a nun. A sign read that it closed at 4.00 pm on Saturdays.

Just then, we saw a man and two women leaving through the door of a side building, an office perhaps, on the cathedral grounds.

'Excuse me!' Paul called out, running up to them. 'Are either of you two ladies a nun?'

The abrupt question took me by surprise since they certainly weren't dressed like nuns.

'Uh, no,' came the reply from one of the women. 'Can we help you with anything?'

'Yes, we are trying to find a nun,' was Paul's response. He was so used to carrying out odd requests for Harry that he offered no further explanation, but I felt obliged to provide some background to our unusual request on a Saturday evening.

'Our son Harry was just watching a little video about a nun, and he was hoping to meet one in person.'

The man smiled kindly at Harry who was holding up his Bun-Bun, not to show to these strangers but to enable Bun-Bun to observe the conversation. He was hopping around with impatience from one foot to another, desperately waiting for something to happen.

'There was a nun here earlier today, but I think you're out of luck for the rest of the weekend I'm afraid.'

'Are you from out of town?' asked one of the women.

'Yes, we're from Melbourne. It's the kids' first time away from home.' I was still embarrassed and keen to move on from the conversation about the nuns.

'Oh! You should go to Sovereign Hill. The kids will love it there!'

Harry suddenly piped up and directed a question at the woman. 'Will there be any nuns there?'

'Oh, there will be many more fun things there than nuns,' said the woman, perhaps realising there was more to the comical situation than met the eye. 'You can pan for gold or go underground into the mines.'

Harry didn't look convinced that this could be better than meeting a nun. The trio eventually wished us luck in our elusive search and said goodbye. Harry continued holding Bun-Bun outstretched in the dark until the three of them had turned the corner and were out of sight.

Back in the apartment that night, there was great excitement about sleeping somewhere other than home for the first time. Scrambling to rescue our first holiday from becoming a disastrous failed attempt at finding a nun, I encouraged Harry to turn his obsessive quest into a fun game. Tessa also got into the game of "scary nun" that Harry had made up, and they took turns at creeping up on each other with a towel draped over their heads, the other person screaming with excited anticipation each time they switched turns. This wasn't an ideal activity leading into bedtime, but it did help divert Harry's focus. The unfortunate consequence was that the kids absconded from their bedrooms repeatedly and rendezvoused around the apartment until

11.00 pm, then slept poorly and woke early, probably due to fears about the scary nun.

The next morning, we stepped into an olden world at Sovereign Hill that was ripe for role play. I had convinced Harry to come along, even though I was unable to promise him a nun that day, on the basis that I would take him to a convent when we got back to Melbourne. The replica settlement was filled with gold rush shopfronts. Actors walked around as gold prospectors and troopers. We panned for gold, wandered through the tents at Government Camp, the base for troopers maintaining law and order over the settlement, and rode on a horse-drawn coach.

Harry was threatened with arrest by a trooper, which he appeared both terrified and pleased about—he enjoyed being singled out for special treatment, even if that involved an intimidating bearded man in uniform with a firearm and handcuffs shouting at him. Eventually, he became upset about the amount of mud stuck to his boots from the unpaved walking paths and Tessa was feeling tired after a poor night's sleep. We decided to conclude the trip before things began to decline. We both agreed it had been a success rescued from the jaws of defeat.

That first trip paved the way for other short trips over the following year. The kids flew on a plane for the first time to visit Tasmania, and we drove to the snowfields to teach them to ski. Each time, we wrestled with whether to go or not, then we wrestled huge amounts of luggage to get there—mainly inordinate amounts of toys that would help maintain Harry's routine for the modest trips of never more than two nights. We were limited to accommodation with ovens and locations where we could source his chicken tenders. We came up with complex plans to maintain Harry's routine, only to be ambushed by him taking an interest in the darndest things that threw the entire routine into chaos. Holidays were tortuous experiences for Paul and me. We were managing an overstimulated autistic child without all our usual infrastructure. Paul would spend most of the drive back home summarising and reiterating reasons why we had reached the holiday quota for the year, glancing at me in the rear-vision mirror as he made his point, while I sat in the back as a physical barrier between the two children. But our efforts were cherished, and they set me free from the guilt that somehow Tessa was missing out. The kids recalled the holidays fondly and liked to list out all the places they had been to, competing with each other to see who could reel off the very short list most accurately. Five years earlier, I had fantasised grandly about dropping off the kids at a ski school while we went ski touring in the French Alps, or camping in the wilds of Wyoming. I had since recalibrated my dreams and concluded that what we were trying to do for the moment seemed to be adventure enough.

MY LIFE'S GREAT WORK

It was March 2023 and Harry had been on a low dose of fluoxetine for the last four weeks. Fluoxetine is an anti-depressant for adults but is often successfully used for treating anxiety in children. We had seen a paediatrician earlier in the year to discuss what medical options there were to try to further take the edge off Harry's anxiety. We still worried that the pace of his progress, although pleasing, wasn't quite enough for him to make a comfortable start at school the following year. Now in his second and final year at kinder, he was still clingy to his BTs, even if he did manage to complete part of the day on his own.

ABA had introduced a token chart reward system in his sessions a few months earlier, and we were using it throughout the day to motivate Harry to push through anxiety-driven barriers. Token charts were touted as another one of the positive behaviour strategies that were not supposed to work for PDA due to the deferred receipt of the reward. The cumulative effect of needing to perform ten individual desirable behaviours to collect ten tokens before obtaining a reward was believed to magnify the size of the demand.

It was true that when rewards were first introduced, they needed to be immediate and tangible to work for Harry. Any delay in their receipt could itself cause a meltdown. I initially was not optimistic about the token system, but over time, Harry became used to the idea of first doing as he was asked and then being rewarded for it. With a lot of practice, he accepted the process and was able to slowly extend the time to final gratification. He was four and a half years old and was able to understand the difference between quantity and quality. We promised him better rewards through the use of tokens.

Many skills ended up being acquired in great surges through our ability to quickly reinforce them with tokens, which was far easier to do than carrying around rewards. However, unknown to us, his general anxiety remained high. In early toddlerhood, the anxiety had been easy to pinpoint. It was unmistakably displayed as refusal, which we had seen less of recently, so assumed that the anxiety had subsided. Now we were looking at controlling behaviour and obsessive-compulsive tendencies which were, in fact, driven by the anxiety. The way he expressed his anxiety had changed as he had grown, and it took us some time to make the association. Every few weeks, new anxiety-driven behaviours cropped up. His repetitive, full-body wiping habit over dinner had materialised out of nowhere just weeks earlier and progressed until he was supervising me wiping down the dining table and chairs prior to him getting seated for dinner, only to immediately start wiping himself before he had taken a bite of anything.

On a trip to the beach, he had screamed about sand getting into his Crocs and he had been unable to even walk along a concrete footpath that cut across the beach due to the presence of windswept sand on it. Every few weeks, new remedial programs needed to be added into his therapy, or creative workarounds had to be developed by us at home. It was exhausting cataloguing it all and coming up with solutions for each of them. We were reluctant to medicate him at such a young age, but we also wanted to tackle the root cause of his challenging behaviours, which was evidently the anxiety, so that we wouldn't have to slap on a Band-Aid or build complex individual solutions using ABA each time, only to have a new one come up.

The paediatrician suggested a low dose of fluoxetine. Given Harry's severe oral sensory aversion, I did not like our chances of getting him to swallow a tablet daily. If he liked chocolate, I could have crushed it up and stirred it into melted chocolate then reset it, but he generally didn't eat chocolate. Luckily, we found a compounding pharmacy that was able to make the medication into an unflavoured liquid suspension which I diluted into his milk each morning. At a low dose, I could get away with it. For the first few weeks, we noticed no changes in his behaviour even though both Paul and I were waiting for it with great anticipation.

One day, Tineke, who had come to supervise a session, commented that Harry seemed to be in a very cooperative mood for the entire session, obliging with requests for less preferred activities like table time and the food program. Later that week, when I went to pick him up, his kinder teacher made a comment that he had needed very little involvement from the teachers or his BTs that week. Big Tessa, who was soon to graduate from university and become a teacher, attended her last few sessions with him as an aide and reported that he had his best kinder days ever. She had simply faded into the background and taken on the role of a regular teaching assistant, an extra resource for all the children. He hadn't needed her at all.

The first significant behaviour change I observed directly that correlated with the commencement of his medication, was the gradual reduction of his obsessive-compulsive wiping behaviours at the dinner table. I had previously offered him five tokens if he managed to get through half a chicken tender without wiping himself. Seeing that was too hard, I reduced the target to two minutes without wiping, then further reduced that to one minute. The demand of that had still immediately seen a spike in his anxious and resistant behaviour, and he deliberately wiped all over himself and the table and chairs in spiteful retaliation to my offer. But after about four weeks of established fluoxetine use, I noticed him trying hard not to wipe himself. His hand lingered over the wet wipe without using it.

'Look!' he cried proudly one night. 'I have finished my chicken tender, and I haven't wiped myself. Give me five tokens!'

It was true. He held out his hand to show me crumbs stuck to his fingers before he finally wiped them off.

At kinder, the BTs ran a program to get him into the sandpit, and one day when I picked him up, I found him standing in the middle of the sandpit furiously digging a hole, sand sprayed all over his clothes.

'I get a token for coming in here,' he told me.

Most of these non-functional habits which had lasted longer than a few days still required some kind of ABA intervention to break through them, but Harry seemed to be increasingly receptive to absorbing the teachings of ABA and generalising the skills into his daily environment. The medication did seem to be having a positive effect and I prepared myself to receive some respite from the persistent levels of elevated stress in our house.

Tessa and Harry sat at the table with some crayons working on colouring sheets while I prepared dinner. Tessa wanted the green crayon which Harry had just taken and which she hadn't wanted until the very moment Harry took it. She screamed and demanded to get it back.

'Give it, Harry!' she cried.

I looked at Tessa, four years old, in the midst of a full tantrum. Definitely a different beast to a meltdown, but not for a lack of intensity. She may have maintained an awareness of her surroundings, had some degree of control, but damn, she was frightening. I looked at her, my previously faultless toddler, and the irony was not lost on me. Harry had mellowed recently, but Tessa had stepped up to fill the void and ensure that the level of challenging behaviour didn't drop too far below our household's default setting. I looked at Harry watching her but not joining in. He held out the green crayon as a peace offering, but it was too late. It wasn't about the green crayon anymore.

'Well, I guess Tessa doesn't want it then,' he said with an exaggerated adult eye roll and then deliberately returned to his drawing.

The medication wasn't quite a magic pill. It did help behaviours that either we or his BTs were already trying to actively modify, but the benefits plateaued after a few months. Despite increasing the dose, we never got back that initial surge in positive behaviour, although the gains made during that time were not lost and his obsessive-compulsive tendencies didn't get too much in the way of daily living. We had the option to experiment further with other medications in the future if the need arose. But, for the moment, it was useful enough to have isolated and confirmed that his anxiety was a major driver behind his most challenging behaviours.

In May, we bid a teary farewell to Big Tessa. She had been with our family for two years, a much-loved nanny, an aide, a trusted friend. Big Tessa was naturally possessed of the kind of warmth and patience I had to take a deep breath and mentally prepare myself to feign each day. She had played a formidable part in Harry's development, bridged the gap between us and his place in the world unaided. Had she not finished her degree and been ready for a full-time job, I doubt we would have let her go. We would have found something for her to do, so afraid we were to let go of anyone who Harry trusted and welcomed into his world as completely as he had done with her. But, as it happened, we took Big Tessa's departure as an opportunity to introduce Harry to doing a complete day at kinder on his own.

We explained to Harry how Big Tessa had gone to school then uni and diligently learnt the things she needed to so that she could do an important job teaching other children. He now no longer needed her but could instead see her from time to time as a friend. He would still get a BT to go with him for a few hours on the other days, but his great gift back to Big Tessa would be to show her that he had learnt all the things they had once done together and could now go to kinder by himself on Mondays.

The ABA therapists had set his kinder up with a rewards chart to keep Harry on track at the times when he was without his safe person. Rather than having to exhaustively specify what he needed to accomplish that day, or to ensure that I had a new reward each time I picked him up, we arrived at an understanding that if he complied with various tasks requested by his teachers and participated in activities, he could earn tokens throughout the day that would go towards a reward he chose each week.

To start with, he was offered ten tokens simply for attending a day at kinder unaided, which meant he could cash it in for a reward immediately when I picked him up. Over time, we reduced the number of tokens he was awarded until eventually he got just one token for the act of attending kinder unaided, but his teachers could give him tokens for other tasks, or if he was kind or helpful to his peers.

By August 2023, Harry was completing two days a week of kinder unaided, which he was attending willingly and happily. He proudly ran through the door at pickup time waving around a piece of artwork he had made during the day, or thrusting a birthday invitation from one of his classmates into my face and telling me he really wanted to go. He went to the parties and danced with his friends. He passed the parcel and pinned the tail on the donkey or whatever the activity was. He liked to sit with his best friend, a little girl named Clara who he sometimes swapped drawings with or picked a flower for.

The two years of hard work in therapy had paid off. I was looking at an almost fully integrated child who was practically school-ready, who had friends, and even best friends. That was everything I had wanted for him at age five. He still had many rigidities, but they were well managed and didn't impede on his kinder experience or those of the children around him. He didn't like to say "hello" to his teachers upon first arrival in the morning, even if I offered him generous amounts of tokens for it. He instead chose to say it soon after I had left so I would not know he had accomplished the most coveted task of the day. He would later show me his token chart and point out which ones were earned for saying "hello". His lunchbox continued to be a sad state of affairs and he still drank his meal replacement formula out of his baby bottle at age five! Other children brought cupcakes into class to celebrate birthdays. He never ate any, but he always wanted to take one to bring home. He was brilliant yet baffling and these quirks were a necessary part of the experience of being Harry.

Thoughts of what to do about myself filtered back into my mind. The following year, Tessa would be in four-year-old kinder and Harry would be doing prep in primary school, maybe even full time. We had decided against sending him to the local primary school which had over 600 children and whose enrolment coordinator had been impatient to wrap up the call with me when I had rung to talk about Harry's special needs. The private schools nearby were also very large, and we worried that he would find himself lost at lunchtimes when hordes of brash older children took over the lawns. So, we chose a small Catholic primary school whose principal met with Harry and personally walked him through the school grounds to show him things of interest and to meet the prep teacher. The principal knew all her students by name. She asked about each of the plush toys Harry was clutching in his hands at the enrolment interview that day and invited him to tell her about any special skills he had. He proudly replied that he could climb to the top of the adult walls at the climbing gym. The interview was a pleasant experience for him and he later stated that he wanted to go to school there. There would likely be some ABA to fit in around his school hours, but it looked like I was on the verge of getting back almost a full working week.

I had spent four and a half out of almost six years as a full-time carer. Two of those years had been oppressive and unbearable, but over the past eight months, I had fashioned a life that was satisfactory enough. With both Harry and Tessa at kinder, I was left with two days a week where I had a few hours to myself. I had made a routine out of going for a midweek climbing session, visiting the three different supermarkets I needed to for all of Harry's specific foods at a leisurely pace, preparing a dinner in advance. A haircut here, a massage there.

It wasn't exciting, but for two days a week it was peaceful, and I had become peacefully unmotivated.

I could have used that time to study something, perhaps start a graduate diploma. I could have at least followed the current affairs or the business news. I didn't do any of those things. Instead, I had accumulated twenty-four months' worth of subscription climbing and outdoor magazines that all lay unopened, the subscriptions having ended a year earlier. I gradually began to open and read them. I had nothing to show for my spare time and it was bothering me only a little.

Having been largely unproductive for two years, other than in the service of Harry, when I was finally able to do something, I was so unaccustomed to being productive that even the most trivial out-of-the-ordinary tasks produced a sense of indignation that I should have to deal with them. Organising an electrician to fix something or dropping off the car for a service were such apparent complications that I delayed them for months. When I finally scraped together the motivation to deal with one of them, it sent me into a tailspin, needing to recalibrate the remaining twenty-three hours in the day to ensure I could fulfil just one paltry obligation. I had become an expert on Harry. My skills and knowhow in this area were second to none. I observed him, interpreted him, and applied solutions onto him like no one else. The entirety of my mental capacity had been poured into problem solving for Harry, and I was completely inept at everything else.

I caught up with friends. They were all working and raising school-age children. Many of them were managing teams of staff and travelling frequently for work. I couldn't fathom travelling for work. The amount of disruption to our finely tuned routine that would have been caused by two days of interstate travel would have been incomprehensible to the average person. Paul would have had to take time off work. It would have taken days of preparation to set up for it, and days of remedial work in the aftermath to right the mess. I expected to feel envy or wistfulness for everyone else's prolific living, but the hunger had gone. I could barely even relate. I listened to their stories and felt either pride for their achievements or sympathy for their problems, but I was no longer in the game. As humans, we must be ingrained to want what is just beyond our reach, what we can see and almost touch. The things that I once wanted were too far gone. I no longer desired them.

I did still want to work again, but the kind of work I wanted had evolved, and I had completely lost the appetite to be an active participant in the corporate hierarchy. What I needed was to work freelance, in a way that reflected the zero capacity I had for politics or schmoozing. Somewhere along my five-year journey with Harry, I had accepted that I had been bestowed a set of priorities at home that would always far outweigh anything I ever took on again in my career.

What I had once seen as the fight of my life had now come to be my life's great work, to advocate for Harry, to prepare the world to receive him and vice versa. At every transitional stage of life, I knew Harry would have unforeseen difficulties. Still, I did want to say the words, 'Mama is going to work' the way Paul got to do each day, and see the faint looks of awe cross the kids' faces at this mysterious *work* thing that adults went out and did. Where I was once preoccupied with what other people thought of me, I now just worried that my kids thought less of me because they didn't recall a time that I was working.

One day, walking past a strip of shops with Harry, he saw a toy in a window that captured his attention and he begged incessantly to have it. I told him I didn't have the money to buy him a toy that day and it startled me to hear him remark with annoyance, 'Can't you just ask Dada to give you some money? He works.'

I struggled to find the right response for the situation. My efforts, which had been so critical to, and determinative of, his early outcomes were also entirely invisible and conceptually vague to him.

I wanted to give an oration about the value of my unpaid domestic work, performed to the exacting, fickle and arbitrary standards of a small despot who stood just over a metre tall, which freed up Dada to go about his paid work with all his workplace rights and protections, a situation where I had clearly drawn the short straw. Since what Dada earned was the product of both of our efforts, it most certainly was not the case that I should have to ask for an allowance from him! But I swallowed the affront and said, 'We've already spent all of Dada's money for this week. Let's see how we go next week.'

I had come to a place of acceptance about my life, our family and Harry's disability. I wasn't always happy about it. Sometimes I was overwhelmed with sadness about the opportunity cost of this path in life. Sometimes it required me saying or doing things that momentarily grated, but I no longer fought it, and it was no longer a preoccupation to get back to life as I had once planned it to be. It was a great relief to have stopped being such a harsh critic of my own reality.

MAKING PEACE

In September 2023, I left all the PDA forums I had once been a part of. It had been close to two years since I had last contributed anything to any of them, although I did still browse through the posts, right up until that last day, indulging in and savouring the desperation in those messages. They reminded me of how far we had come, and I didn't ever want to forget that. I shared so much common ground with these strangers, but it was a common ground that had become divided by a deep chasm.

In the last two years, my experiences on the forum had been frustrating. Daily, sometimes multiple times daily, a forlorn and anguished message from a member would come up in my alerts. *We have tried everything, psychology, OT and music therapy. We have a low-demand household. She is home-schooled, but she will not let me leave the house. My husband does not agree with this approach, and we are talking about separation. Does anyone have any advice on what else to try?* Sometimes, the messages were adrenalin-fuelled, typed as a meltdown was taking place. *I am currently locked in my bedroom and have been for the past hour. I filled up the wrong water bottle and he had a meltdown. I tried to give him the right water bottle, but he wouldn't take it and now he is kicking holes in the wall. What will happen if I call the police?*

I had read these misery-laden stories and volunteered my own, a variant that held hope. It is often the case that people take to the online world when they are at their lowest. They share their darkest stories, but do not come back to inform their audience when things improve, probably because they are off doing better things than moping around online. I recall at the start of our journey, desperately searching through the posts, scrolling back years, looking for even just one happy story from someone who had succeeded in some small way. With that in mind, I chose to share. I told them about ABA.

Having seen other threads about ABA get shut down, the handful of times I had found the courage to mention it, I had approached it tentatively, giving examples of how it had worked for Harry. I thought I had employed enough diplomacy that an inquisitive discussion might follow, or that individual members might message me in private for further information, but that was never the case. The responses were fiery and critical, and they came on quickly. *I can see that you think that you are helping your son, but you are not. There is a reason why ABA is conducted on such young children.* Or perhaps the most hurtful one I read of all: *ABA is conversion therapy and what you are doing is cruel.* Eventually, a moderator turned off the comments on my post and I never contributed to a forum again. It seemed such a dangerous attitude to adopt, to deny that ABA could be applied in a way that was gentle yet helpful, but I could taste the malice in their comments. I knew this audience was not ready to hear about ABA from one of their peers, not like that.

The forums were also filled with posts from members seeking recommendations of "PDA aware" paediatricians or therapists, of which there were very few in Australia. I had so much I wanted to share on that front, too, that again I withheld. It wasn't that I would have been chastised for it, but because by then I had chosen an approach of silence. I had stopped using the term PDA as a way of centring conversations about Harry with paediatricians and therapists. When I did use the term, I tested it for recognition, and when none came back, I focused instead on describing the behaviours and the pattern of demand avoidance rather than relying on the label.

Did I still believe that PDA was a thing, its own distinct subtype on the autism spectrum? Yes, unequivocally so. There was a reason why I gravitated towards the PDA forums rather than the general autism forums. Nevertheless, I had decided that the lack of formal recognition of PDA did not necessarily prevent Harry from receiving effective treatment for his condition, so long as we sought out the help of professionals who were open-minded and inquiring. It was possible for a treating professional to be hearing about PDA for the first time and still find an effective treatment. With each new treating professional, I made sure to say that I really thought Harry fit within the PDA profile. Sometimes I got no discernible response, but it seemed important to give it that kind of validation anyway. I trust that over time, repeated exposure to patients and clients like Harry, and the prevalence of stories like this one, will eventually see a professional recognition of the subtype in Australia. I am hopeful that the plight of the next generation of PDAers will be more readily understood, and their treatment options more widely available.

One area where I strongly felt that recognition of PDA would be particularly useful was in an educational context, since the teaching strategies which proved effective for Harry really did need to be much more creative and collaborative than for other children. In 2022, we enrolled both children in swim classes at a place called The Little Swim School that was particularly experienced in teaching children with disabilities. For months, Harry's swim teacher, Jess, patiently asked him to put on goggles, which he staunchly refused. He didn't like the tightness of the goggles pressed against his head and face. He didn't like what they were supposed to enable him to do—put his head underwater—because he didn't like his hair getting wet. There was so much for Harry to dislike about goggles. Jess was experienced with children on the autism spectrum, and she read him well. She pushed a little, then backed off and switched activities when she realised that pushing further would cause him to cease participating altogether.

One class, Jess watched as I lined up three pairs of goggles on the edge of the pool that I had purchased during the week, each with different designs and colours. She added two more that were spares belonging to the swim school.

'Okay, Harry, take your pick,' I said to him, pointing to the five goggles sitting there.

Harry looked at me, then at the goggles and calmly picked up one at a time and threw them into the neighbouring swimming lane.

'Is he PDA?' Jess asked, as she began to steer Harry onto the next activity, realising that goggles weren't going to happen that day.

'Yes!' came my disbelieving reply.

This was the first time since Harry's psychologist had initially mentioned PDA two and a half years ago that anyone had independently identified Harry with this obscure condition.

'I've just learnt about it. We have two others here who might be PDA,' she said. 'So, what works for Harry? What do they do in ABA?'

'They do a lot of role play in his therapy,' I said. 'They use his favourite characters to make a bit of a story and get him to do tasks as part of the story.'

Jess listened carefully. She had previously, upon our advice, tried to motivate him by using pool toys that were a bit of a novelty, things like an assortment of floating toy poop that she got him to collect on the kickboard while swimming around. They had all worked to an extent, but ceased once the level of difficulty increased and the novelty wore off.

The following week when we turned up, Jess had made waterproof, laminated flashcards using various Harry Potter characters, which could be matched up with swimming-related flashcards depicting specific tasks, such as kicking while on one's back, blowing bubbles in the water and putting on goggles. The idea was that Harry could choose a Harry Potter character and the swimming task that had been assigned to that character would be revealed.

Suddenly Harry was interested. He wanted to see the flashcards, and he grinned until his dimples glistened in the water. From a PDAer's perspective, there were a multitude of reasons why this approach was acceptable when the usual one was not, even though he was being asked to perform exactly the same task. First, it was not Jess telling him to put on his goggles, it was some unknown force with which he was not engaged in a power struggle. Harry was not happy to be ordered around by a person, but by random chance, that was okay. Second, the surprise element was a novelty, as was this new game. Third, it involved his special interest area. When the flashcard for putting on goggles came around, he hesitated, but Jess was one step ahead. She must have spent the week watching Harry Potter movies.

'Oh, how exciting!' she cried. 'This is just like the challenge in the Goblet of Fire when Harry goes underwater to rescue his friends.'

She dropped a few sinkable toys into the shallow water.

'Let's pretend this one is Hermione, and that one is Ron,' she said. 'Now, when you put on your goggles, you will be able to see them under the water. Who are you going to rescue first?'

'Hermione,' shouted Harry excitedly after letting Jess put the goggles on him. Then he plunged his head under, submerging it fully in the shallow water, and brought up one of the sinkable toys.

Until that day, Harry had been stalled at the same level in his swimming progression for over six months. We had persisted with coming to class every week because staying at that level was still better than going backwards and losing familiarity with water. The day the Harry Potter flashcards were introduced, he progressed further in ten minutes than he had in a full year of swim classes.

Jess had done her research and unlocked the secret to teaching a PDAer. She was now armed with a template that she could possibly reuse with her two other PDA clients. Even within our little world, we could see that awareness about PDA was spreading. We did not have the benefit of the widespread knowledge that came with it being a recognised condition. But when we found the right people, and it seemed there were more of these people to find than I had first expected, it proved to be rewarding to put in the work to educate them about PDA and break the trail for the next generation.

EPILOGUE

You started prep earlier this year, in a small primary school five minutes' walk from home. A few weeks shy of your sixth birthday, on your very first day of school, you walked into the classroom with a smile, without an aide or a broomstick, wearing a pair of stiff new school shoes that I had secretly been softening with a hammer in the preceding weeks. Two years earlier, I would have considered this scenario more far-fetched than a wizarding fantasy.

I know there will be certain settings at school, now and in the coming years, that are likely to be problematic for you. Sport class. How will you cope with the pointed demand of ball handling drills, or the cooperation required for a game of tunnel ball? Lunchtimes. Will you be teased about the baby food in your lunch box, or the bottle of milk that we send along with you? School camps. Can you cook a chicken tender over a campfire? I have no idea how we will navigate these issues, but I'm trying my best to practise the art of leaving it to be worked out closer to the time, because you have changed so much in such a short time. For now, I am riding a wave of relief that school is going well, and that you do so few hours of therapy, that in a few short weeks I will be returning to work as a lawyer.

At every stage of our journey, most of my expectations and worries about you have been proven wrong. Yet I wonder if things had been left to their own devices, whether I would have been that far off the mark. I am sure my inclination to catastrophise, to plan for the worst-case scenario and to exhaustively pursue each possible solution, are to blame for much of the tension that pervaded our household over the two years of the pandemic where you, my atypical and misunderstood toddler, were trapped. Yet, if it has also played a role in your success so far, then every moment of that struggle was worthwhile, and nothing was in vain. I wish only that my mind had not been so closed off to all the potential that I could not see at the time, for I may have emerged from this experience far less wounded.

I wonder whether that magnificent memory of yours stretches far back enough to recall the kindness and commitment that we were met with in the years soon after your diagnosis. The teachers and therapists and other parents who, once told of your autism, looked for ways to include and welcome you. All those play dates where other parents made the effort to plant some toys that suited your special interests, and parties where they made sure there was something you could eat. Their actions caused me more than once to reflect upon myself, and wonder whether I, in their situation, not charged with the responsibility of raising an autistic child of my own, would have had the compassion to do the same.

Of all the decisions we faced in those early days, the one that came most intuitively and easily was to embrace your diagnosis, to tell people all about you. Yes, we encountered ignorance, but for the most part, people were interested and wanted to learn more. When we were open to share, they were open to receive, and I was humbled time and again by the amount of goodwill that came from unexpected places. I talk about you a lot these days, maybe because it is what I feel I can contribute to this community that we are now a part of—the disability community, the neurodivergent community. I meet someone new and find myself in a hurry to share that I am the parent of a child on the spectrum. I want to speak of these epic five years that have been agonising and wretched, hilarious and triumphant. I am a champion of your special brand of autism.

Epilogue

I have received a hard-earned moment of reprieve. Things are pretty good right now, but I understand that progress is not linear. Certain milestones—the advent of puberty, a first crush, a change of schools, a job—I expect that all those moments will be a source of setbacks and challenges and my problem-solving skills will again be called back into service. I have found my calling, an authentic one, where my role is indispensable and where I have no choice other than to find a way to succeed.

Your days of ABA may soon be coming to a close. Tineke once said that one of the problems they frequently encountered was when it came time to tell parents that ABA was no longer needed. Indeed, we shall find it very hard to let go of these people who, for the past few years, have been intimately entwined in our lives, the only other people to know you as we do. In the fullness of time, you can tell me what you thought of it all, but in my eyes, your therapists have done an almighty job. They lifted layers and layers of dysfunction to reveal an astonishing and unique individual. They looked for and found bountiful stores of abilities when your own parents were too burnt-out, overwhelmed, and clueless about autism to know where to begin. Contrary to my fears that lurked in the background, they did not crush your spirit. They brought it out, roaring like the Hulk and soaring like Harry Potter.

There may come a time in your life when you question your place in the world. It must be the silent fear of everyone who has parented an autistic child that they may not be around for when that moment comes. My great hope for you is that by then you will have come to your own realisation that incredible minds do not think alike, they think differently. I invite you to read this book. Even in the hardest moments, you will see that we have always found somewhere for you to meet the world halfway. A place that brought out your brilliant, creative best.

Do you remember all those years we shouted out the magical code words that you gave to us, 'Harry Potter gets his hair wet!', as the fix for when you got your hair splashed in the bath? Or the suitcase that you wheeled into kinder because you refused to carry your own backpack, and it made all the other kids want a suitcase too? You've done different since the day you were born. You own different. You make everyone else want to be different. Your fierce little sister has spent her entire short life chasing the dream of doing 'the same as Harry', her steadfast tormentor and her adored hero.

You may be our child on the spectrum, the one with special needs, but the once incessant question of *whether* you will be able to do something has been replaced by *how* you will go about doing it. It has become a source of curiosity, rather than one of despair, as we wait to see what on earth you will come up with next. Whatever chaos you caused, or problem you solved, you have always done it in the most fascinating way.

I hope you already know from having seen the tireless attempts we made to first try to understand and accommodate you, then to encourage and guide you, and finally to foster and let unfold the beguiling riddle that you are, how much you are loved. We may have started out as an odd and incompatible pairing for a mother and a child, since I was once devastatingly efficient, and you the master of procrastination. Yet somewhere along the way, I came to understand that I had been given a challenge harder than I could have ever imagined, to fulfil a purpose in life greater than I would otherwise have known. For someone who was driven but directionless, that has been one extraordinary gift.

ACKNOWLEDGEMENTS

I did not originally set out to write a book. I set out to record our family's story so that in my old age I would never forget what we lived through. As a result, I wrote this memoir in secret for much of the process. The first person to discover what I was doing was my husband, Paul, who has supported me on the road to publication since. The words may be mine, but the story is ours. I am incredibly lucky to have you as my partner on life's journey.

A staggering number of people have been part of Team Harry over the years. This story is a triumphant one because of their work. Thank you to our team members at Happy Oak Behavioural Consulting. This book is my five-star Google review for their life-changing work. I am forever grateful to Tineke Sibbel and Sarah Scambler for their understanding and willingness to tackle anything. Special mention to Stephanie Stewart, Tori Cason, Rachel Alwyn, Tahlia Tucker, Jemma Singleton, Tia Rodrigues, Helena Granada, Jennifer Wild, Paige McCubbin, Chloe Lim, Teresa Lamanna and Phebe Tan who each worked with our family for extensive periods of time.

Heartfelt thanks to the following people who have played a significant role in Harry's development over the period covered in this memoir:

Tessa Jones, who is forever immortalised in these pages as Big Tessa. I am reminded of you whenever I look at Harry and you hold a very special place in our hearts.

Karen Szabo, Anne Thiel, Lily Li and Lee Mohtaji at Canterbury Gardens Kindergarten, for their quiet confidence and kind reassurance.

Joanna Butchart, our favourite "aunty", for stepping up to a special role and for being a ready presence in our lives.

Jessica Parker and Sarah Melin, for pointing us in the direction of ABA.

Sonali and Ben Zanatta, and Liam and Natalie Gilchrist for the years of friendship and for sticking with us through those tricky early playdates.

Jess Adkins-Barber at The Little Swim School for her creativity and persistence.

Grandma, Grandpa, Nana and Pa, for grandparenting in a way I'm sure they never expected to.

Grateful acknowledgement to the following people who have supported me:

Chad Heazlewood who read an early excerpt of this book and gave me the confidence to pursue this with the same gusto that he sandbags every climb.

Nanae Hill, Susie Grehl, Amanda Chew, Inaya Bryne, Priya Diaz, Wendy Ng, Edwina Smith, Lauren Butchart, Dora Guslitser, Sofie Dieu and Neil McCann for giving me considered feedback over various title and cover concepts.

Danielle Nahum, friend, boss and person who makes things happen, for extending a helping hand in my return to working life while enthusiastically supporting this book.

Hawkeye Publishing for running their unpublished manuscript prize in fierce support of fresh voices. Without this vote of confidence I might still be sitting on this manuscript, wondering if I was deluded in thinking it publishable.

Camille Booker, Anne Freeman, and Andy McCarthy, for carving out time from their young families to read this book and lend their words of endorsement. Camille did so while preparing for the launch of her much anticipated *The Woman in the Waves*, Anne while writing her third book, the evocatively titled, *The Time After Now*, and Andy while on the road promoting his uplifting debut, *Here Comes the Sun*. Their kindness, which came right as I approached the pointy end of the publishing process, has left an indelible mark upon me.

Nicole Rogerson, Dr Sally Munday, Dr Erin Leif and Craig Salisbury, each of whom in their line of work routinely see families like mine at their most vulnerable; who understood the value of sharing this story, and gave their time to read and endorse it. These are individuals who know that the story in this book is not a rare one, only a poorly understood one. Thank you for your part in helping this book get into the hands of those who might find the hope they need in it.

Julia Ferracane of Righteous PR, for her wisdom, her little black book and her willingness to understand this story so deeply.

Natasha Gilmour, my delightful publisher at The Kind Press, for recognising the value of this story and plucking it out of the wilderness. Thank you for taking care of my little book.

To my squeaky little Tessa, who was aggrieved to learn that this book is mainly about Harry. You should know that in those darkest days, you were the reason I kept putting one foot in front of the other.

Finally, to Harry ... it is my greatest honour to be on Team Harry.

ABOUT THE AUTHOR

PORSCIA LAM

Porscia Lam is a Melbourne lawyer who has spent over fifteen years working in large firms and financial institutions. In 2021, she began a three-year career break to care for two young children, one of whom was diagnosed with Autism Spectrum Disorder.

During this time, Porscia immersed herself in learning about autism, Pathological Demand Avoidance and ABA therapy. The success of her son's early intervention therapy led her to write her first book, *The Unlocking: An Autism Story,* which was shortlisted for the Hawkeye Manuscript Development Prize in 2024.

In her spare time, Porscia is a keen rock-climber and occasionally contributes articles to outdoor magazines and blogs.

@porscialam
porscialam.com

www.ingramcontent.com/pod-product-compliance
Lightning Source LLC
Chambersburg PA
CBHW060600080526
44585CB00013B/637